Communication knowledge and the librarian

K J McGARRY
Principal Lecturer
College of Librarianship Wales

CLIVE BINGLEY LINNET BOOKS
LONDON HAMDEN · CQNN

FIRST PUBLISHED 1975 BY CLIVE BINGLEY LTD
16 PEMBRIDGE ROAD LONDON W11
SIMULTANEOUSLY PUBLISHED IN USA BY LINNET BOOKS
AN IMPRINT OF THE SHOE STRING PRESS INC
995 SHERMAN AVENUE HAMDEN CONNECTICUT 06514
SET IN 10 ON 12 POINT PRESS ROMAN
PRINTED AND BOUND IN THE UK BY
REDWOOD BURN LIMITED TROWBRIDGE AND ESHER
COPYRIGHT © K J MCGARRY 1975
ALL RIGHTS RESERVED
CLIVE BINGLEY ISBN: 0–85157–188–3
LINNET BOOKS ISBN: 0–208–01369–3

Library of Congress Cataloging in Publication Data

McGarry, K   J
    Communication knowledge and the librarian.

    Bibliography: p.
    Includes index.
    1.   Communication.   2.   Libraries.   I.   Title.
P90.M238   001.5   75–4864
ISBN 0–208–01369–5

Contents

TO, CELIA AIDAN AND RUTH

PREFACE

THE PRIMARY OBJECTIVE of this book is to examine three interrelated concepts and present them as an attempted synthesis for a foundation study for librarianship. It is the product of some years planning and teaching foundation courses and special papers in communication studies at the College of Librarianship Wales, and the Postgraduate School of Library Studies at McGill University, Montreal.

The secondary objective is to put forward the view that it is not enough for teachers and students of librarianship to ask such questions as: 'What is the structure of librarianship?' and 'How is this structure maintained?' We must also try and explain the social role of our profession in terms of other related studies, particularly those concerned with human behaviour and with the analysis of society. Librarianship can never be adequately explained in terms of itself alone.

The bias of this work is therefore sociological and behavioural; it attempts to analyse at an introductory level the information-seeking behaviour of man; the nature of the interpersonal communication situation; how men communicate within groups; how human groups communicate with each other, and the degree to which this total complex of interaction produces the communications and knowledge systems of society. It is hoped that we can then ask: 'How did such patterns emerge?'; 'How are they changing?' and 'What are the implications of these changes for librarianship?'.

The emphasis throughout the work is on the importance of the inter-personal situation and the communication problems it introduces. Librarianship, if it is a profession at all, is a 'personal service profession', and one which will become increasingly significant in the society of the future—which, the economists tell us, will see the growth of services and a diminution in the importance of goods. In such a new-style service economy, knowledge will be the key to power and survival. It follows then that the art of interpersonal communication is a valid study for the librarian for two major reasons. The end product of all our techniques is the enquiry—encounter with other human beings.

Indeed, as an educational objective we should keep in mind not whether a student will be a good administrator, cataloguer or technologist, but how will the curriculum help him or her to cope effectively in a professional—client situation.

The second reason is that we have in the past given insufficient thought to the relationships between interpersonal communication behaviour and man's systems of recorded knowledge. We have tended to tackle the universe of recorded thought head-on, without regard to its dependence upon the many networks of our social communication systems. I believe that if we examine the intricate relationships between society, communication and knowledge that we shall get at least tentative answers to our own professional problems, their genesis and development, and we may even get a glimpse of our professional future—for we are educating students who will be practising professionals in the twenty-first century.

The selection of themes for treatment is largely personal, and where possible I have used communication models to impose structure on the material. I am acutely aware that I have sometimes skated over issues and problems which are highly complex, and in part compensation the book includes notes and references which may encourage others to dig more deeply.

K J McGARRY

CHAPTER 1

Communication:
definitions and models

CONSCIOUSLY OR UNCONSCIOUSLY we have been studying communication all our lives. From the time when as small babies we became aware that the responses of our parents could be controlled by cries and gurgles, and later by the use of certain sounds, we seemed to know innately that communication was essential for our survival.

Our existence depends on communication in more ways that we can easily enumerate. Without our initial backlog of genetic messages we would not be who we are, and without the internal communication system of our bodies we could not live and function as we do. Living, therefore, is largely a matter of communicating and many people make their living by communicating with others: broadcasters, politicians, advertisers, teachers—and librarians who are involved in communiction in a special way. Although it is one of the most frequently used words in the English language we find it very difficult to come up with a finely calibrated definition of communication that will please everybody. Surely, it may be said, you must already know what communication is before you can profitably attempt to define or discuss it. And of course there is a sense in which we do know what it is. We know how to use the word correctly and we understand the word when we hear it used. Yet most of us when confronted with a request for a definition would be inclined to reply, like St Augustine, 'I know so long as you don't ask me'. The etymology of the term gives us very little help, coming from the Latin, *communicare* it gives us an idea of 'sharing' and is related to such terms as 'communion', 'commune' and 'communist'. Perhaps the real trouble is that when we try to define communication we are faced with the problem that the term we are about to describe must also be used in the discussion and so we are continually being forced to stand in our own shadow. Much the same

7

problem applies to such questions as 'What is freedom?', What is intelligence?', and 'What is life?'. This problem of definition highlights the relationship between the field of communication and the problem of human knowledge. If we were asked to define librarianship we might say that it is an activity concerned with the acquisition, organization and dissemination of recorded knowledge which is saying what it *does* rather than what it is. Perhaps an acceptable definition of librarianship might not be of much help even if it were obtainable. We need an explanation rather than a definition, a detailed account of the work the concept has to do, an idea of the meaning that the term librarianship evokes in others, and an idea of the territory it is supposed to cover. Having done this we might at least be able to say what librarianship is *not* which is just as important as being able to say what it is. In order to find out what something is we try to demarcate its area of application — an enterprise even more difficult for communication than for librarianship.

If we look at the field of human knowledge we find that some subjects are more easily demarcated than others. Geology, for instance is concerned with the history and structure of the earth's crust, chemistry is the science concerned with the composition of matter and of the changes that take place in it under varying conditions. Both subjects have reasonably defined areas of application and there is a general agreement among geologists and chemists as to the nature and scope of their respective studies. Those subjects which deal with man and his behaviour, such subjects as philosophy and sociology, are less easily defined and there is often a multiplicity of viewpoints as to the nature of the subject. The same is true of communication.

1.1 THE DIVERSITY OF PERSPECTIVES
Although the problems of communication must be as old as Homo Sapiens the idea of communication as a discipline is comparatively modern. The first systematic treatment was given by Aristotle (1) who developed what came to be known as the study of rhetoric, which dealt with the stratagems and ploys of public speaking and for more than two thousand years this study was to provide the main axioms and rules for the arts of communication. There are now, however, many disciplines declaring a stake in the problems of human communication; indeed it could be said that communication

8

in all its many facets has succeeded those twin pillars of science: biology and physics as the major study of our time. But in my father's house there are many mansions and Franklin Knower (2) lists more than twenty disciplines which provide some conceptual or methodological approach to the subject. This list is extended by Erwin Bettinghaus (3) who claims to have isolated fifty definitions each reflecting a completely different subject approach to the topic.

In order to give us an overview of the differing approaches to communication we could use as a framework the main classes of the Dewey decimal classification scheme: philosophy, religion, the social sciences, language, science, technology, the arts, literature and history. Within each of these major fields and their constituent sub-fields are specialists and scholars who view the problems of communication in different ways.

In the first two main classes we encounter the interests of the philosopher and theologian. The dominant approach to-day is seen in the writings of the existentialists, and the prime exemplar is Karl Jaspers (4), who regards communication as the universal condition of man's being; a problem which is discussed in greater depth by the Jewish theologian Martin Buber (5) who concentrates on the problems of communication from the religious standpoint.

Both Buber and Jaspers emphasise that the use of communication is to 'commune' not to 'command' and they reject the traditional epistemological doctrine that true understanding is gained by objectivity alone. On the contrary they assert that 'empathy' and 'inter-subjectivity' are the keystones of the communicative act, a theory that has had a strong influence on psychiatry and theology, and is embodied in the writings of Paul Tillich (6) and Joost Meerloo (7). When we turn to the social sciences we find that communication and culture are treated as synonymous by many scholars. Indeed, E T Hall (8) begins chapter four of his classic work with the assertion that 'communication is culture'.

The concept of society as a network of relationships between individuals and groups receives detailed treatment in the writings of Muzafar Sherif (9) and Wilbur Schramm (10). Again at the other end of the spectrum we have the works of empirical and rationalist philosophers, ranging from the analytical philosophy of A J Ayer (11) to the linguistic constructs of Benjamin Lee Whorf (12) and the revolutionary upheavals in psycholinguistics caused by the writings of Noam Chomsky (13). The physical sciences contribute to

9

communication largely in the form of technical subfields bearing such important headings as cybernetics, a science launched by the researches of W Ross Ashby and Norbert Wiener, information theory which is much indebted to the classic work of Claude Shannon (14) and Warren C Weaver, and general system theory which is largely the brainchild of Ludwig von Bertalanffy (15).

The communications revolution has not only proceeded by historical stages, but seems to have exploded simultaneously on several plateaus of thought. The technologist is busy demonstrating the fact that his craft has transformed the media of communication from telegraph and television to satellite communication, and the historian has to consider the causal connexions between communications technology and social change: a problem not without relevance for the development of librarianship. Other approaches to communication cross the traditional boundaries of psychology and sociology and are represented by journalism, rhetoric and political science.

The humanities, as traditionally conceived, provide a rich legacy of precept and practice for the communicative arts. For I A Richards (16), the arts represent the 'supreme form of the communicative activity', and for another critic F R Leavis (17) 'poetry can communicate the quality of experience with a subtlety unapproached by any other means'. The historian has traditionally envisaged his subject as a dialogue with the past, but now the new communicative dimension of our preliterate past is being opened for us by the archaeologist and the geologist. Nor have the geographers been slow to recognise the value of communication theory for the analysis of the phenomena of urbanism, or in constructing models of urban life as an ongoing flow of communication, always changing because of ever widening settings. A famous demographer, Harvey Cox (18), likens urban life to the activity of a vast complicated switchboard where man is the communicator and the metropolis a vast network of communication possibilities. Richard Meier (19) applies the techniques of cybernetics to the concept of urbanization, regarding the city as an information system with facilities for the storage and production of new information.

From the foregoing variety of perspectives, it can be readily seen how difficult it would be to find an agreed definition of communication—much less attempt a synthesis which would be satisfactory for every specialist. Again, as T R Nilson (20) points out, it is impossible to draw the line between those situations we conventionally describe as communication and those we do not. Because of this fact a notable feature of the literature is the popularity of selected readings, which attempt an overview of the whole range of communication. One outstanding example of this kind of publication is that of Floyd Mateson and Ashley Montague (21). The passages are so selected as to deliberately advance the provocative view that the field of communication is more than ever a battleground between two opposing conceptual forces—those of monologue and those of dialogue. In their estimation, the 'monologic' approach treats communication as essentially the transmission and reception of 'symbolic stimuli' or messages and commands: this view often finds expression in cybernetics, combative game theory and mass persuasion. The 'dialogic' approach is exemplified in religious existentialism, symbolic interaction and any other area of thought which regards communication as a genuine encounter between equals and a quest for understanding.

1.2 DEFINITIONS

T R Nilson (22) classified definitions of communication into two main categories: in one are those definitions which limit the process of communication to those in 'stimulus response' situations, in which one deliberately transmits stimuli to evoke a response. In this situation the communicator acts as a transmission agent in giving a command or in some way attempting to alter the behaviour of the receiver. In the other category, he includes those definitions which include unintentional communication as when one person reacts to another on the detection of some visual, auditory, or any other sensory cue. As Newcomb (23) notes, the man who allows rubbish to accumulate in his backyard communicates something about himself whether he intends to or not. If one looks at some representative dictionary definitions there is a discernible pattern which tends to conform with Mateson's 'monologic' and 'dialogic' communication:
Communication—the imparting conveying or exchanging of ideas and knowledge whether by speech, writing or signs.

Oxford English Dictionary
Communication—the transfer of thoughts and messages as contrasted with the transportation of goods and persons. The basic forms of communication are by signs (sight) and sound (hearing).

Columbia Encyclopaedia

11

These two definitions are based mainly on the idea of the *transfer* of information; they distinguish between the transfer of ideas and the transfer of material things. A newer aspect, which is much indebted to learning theory, gives greater prominence to the concept of *influence* as a necessary criterion of the success of the communicative act; that is, if A communicates with B and B's behaviour is not modified in some way, the communication has *not* taken place; or as Schramm (24) puts it: *A communicates B through channel C to D with effect E.* Another specialist, S S Stevens, using the language of the biologist, develops the same idea:

Communication is the discriminatory response of an organism to a stimulus.... Communication occurs when some environmental disturbance (the stimulus) impinges on the organism and the organism does something about it. If the stimulus has been ignored by the organism, then there has been no communication. The test is the differential reaction of some sort. The message that gets no response is not a communication (25).

In Warren Weaver's definition, the conceptual frame is widened even further to take in the action of machines:
The word communication will be used here in a broad sense to include all of the procedures by which one mind may affect another.... In some connection it may be desirable to use a still broader definition of communication to include the procedures by which one mechanism (say automatic equipment to track an aeroplane and compute its probable future positions) affects another mechanism, say a guided missile chasing this aeroplane (26).

The principal objection which a behavioural scientist might lodge against these definitions is their unwarranted emphasis on linearity. Someone or something does something to somebody or something else. No account is taken of interaction: the fact that the recipient of the communication might have an influence upon the communicator, or that there might be any sense of *sharing* is ignored or considered of secondary importance only. Charles Morris, the famous semanticist, gives another definition which stresses the interactive properties of the communication situation.
The term communication when widely used covers any instance of the establishment of a commonage, that is the making common of some property of a number of things. In this sense a radiator 'communicates' its heat to surrounding bodies, and whatever

medium serves this process of making common is a means of communication (the air, a road, a telegraph system). For our purposes 'communication' will be limited to the use of signs to establish a commonage of signification—whether by signs or by other means and this we shall call communication (27).

Morris recognises that the term 'communication' is extensive enough to cover the communication of heat by radiators or the communications provided by roads, railways *etc.* But these are *channels*, that is a second order form of communication, and 'commonage' as Morris sees it, is only established when symbols are used to establish what he calls a 'common mental orientation' towards a particular field of reference, say a common problem or any act which may result in a decision. In other words, when the agents in the act of communication are self-reflective as well as self-monitoring. This limiting of communication to the conscious use of signs and symbols is endorsed by the sociologist George Lundberg:

We shall use communication to designate interaction by means of signs and symbols. The symbols. The symbols may be gestural, pictorial, plastic or verbal or any other which would serve as stimuli to behaviour.... Communication is therefore a sub-category under interaction, namely the form of interaction which takes place through symbols (28).

Lundberg goes on to add that this definition is subject to certain qualifications, for instance, we must distinguish between communication and mere *contact*; true societal communication consists in temporarily identifying oneself with the other person in the use of the symbols which serve as a basis for the act of communication.

But as yet, no general comprehensive definition has been put forward which gives us any idea of the social function of communication, or the relationship between the interpersonal communication act and the function of communication within society. It is generally agreed among sociologists that the *locus classicus* for this statement lies in the definition by Charles Cooley:

By communications is here meant the mechanism through which all human relations exist and develop—all the symbols of the mind together with the means of conveying through space and preserving them in time....(29)

This is a broad concept of communication and one which is of demonstrable relevance for the sociology of librarianship: a

13

profession engaged in the preservation and dissemination of symbols whether, in Lundberg's terms, they are plastic, visual or verbal or any other, acting as a channel in the process of communication. Edward Sapir (30), in defining communication, wrote of 'explicit' and 'implicit' communication. 'Explicit' communication is concerned mainly with the use of language to gain a common understanding among people; 'implicit' communication is the unconscious assimilation by the individual of the ideas beliefs and values of his culture and the way in which they influence his behaviour and attitudes.

In summarizing the underlying points of the definitions discussed, it emerges that communication is based on a relationship and this relationship may exist between two persons, or between one person and many; between collective society and an individual, and between society and a group. Human beings successfully communicate with each other and with machines and, as Shannon points out in his definition, machines communicate with each other within the limits of the capability designed into them. The essence of this relationship is being *in tune* or focussing on the same information. Cooley's definition emphasises the social function of communication, the ensuring of continuity, the very essence and *sine qua non* of man as a social being. In being able to communicate with the past, an extra dimension is given to the life of a human being; a facility provided for in the organization of knowledge expressed in symbolic form and its conveying through space and preserving in time; as expressed in Cooley's definitive emphasis on the time binding function of social communication. Thus the development of the mass media demonstrated the gradual conquest of space and time, with the library as a partner in freezing in time the legacy of the past; enabling the reader to gain access to the poetry of Homer and the philosophical speculations of Aristotle. In a sense this too is communication, but obviously there are differences in quality between those communication relationships that are close and direct, and those that are removed in time and space; rather like the difference between direct and vicarious experience.

1.3 THE USE OF MODELS

Just as it is said that there is a different definition of art for every artist, so every work on the theory or practice of communication tends to put forward a definition which is usually a variant on some

14

of the standard ones which have been discussed. As communication studies became more and more under the influence of the scientific mode of thinking, the practice grew of analysing what was thought to be the basic components of the communication act, with the intention of detecting barriers to communication and improving efficiency. The concept of 'model' is becoming increasingly adopted in scholarly thought. Its usage crosscuts all the major disciplines, since it operates as a conceptual bridge between theory and fact, the unique and the general, and helps the student organize his object of study.

An example of this approach is the Subject-Object Relations Group, an interdisciplinary seminar representing a wide variety of disciplines which met regularly during 1969-70 at the University of Sheffield (31). Its members investigated the use of models as a remedy for the interdisciplinary problems of scholarly analysis and as a precondition for the advancement and unification of knowledge.

A communication system or model affords the communication scientist a procedure for cutting through the enormous complexity of human interaction. In essence, a model is an analogy or replication of events that attempts to explain the nature of a given set of occurrences. Man is a compulsive model builder and it is this way that he structures his experience and these resultant schema greatly determine his perceptions and his behaviour. Kenneth Boulding (32) calls his social model 'the image', which means 'the sum of what we think we know and what makes us behave the way we do'. The study of this image he calls 'eiconics'.

In his provocative historiography of science, T S Kuhn (33) argues that 'normal science' presupposes a conceptual model or paradigm which is accepted by the scientific community. The location of new facts and problems inevitably evokes crises which cannot be explained by this operational model; and science returns to normal only when the scientific community accepts a new model or structure which can again govern its search for new facts and more refined theories. The history of social change within science is therefore a history of models which have been discarded because some new event has shown up the deficiency in their explanatory powers. Edward de Bono (34) characterises the model as a method of transferring some relationship or process from its actual setting to one where it may be more conveniently studied. In order to study the proportions of Canterbury cathedral we might take a photograph and use it as a basis of study. The photograph is a model of the cathedral even though it is differently shaded areas of paper than now demonstrate the relationships between its components. A better model might be of wood or cardboard which would present the extra dimensions of these relationships. In the same way, a library school lecturer might use a model of a library building to illustrate the conceptual points made in his lecture; and, similarly, a classification scheme attempts to present a working model for the arrangement of recorded knowledge. Like Kuhn's paradigm of scientific change classification schemes become inadequate as new knowledge and new interrelationships between subjects begin to detract from their explanatory powers.

All models involve this transformation of relationships from their original setting into another. Once they have been made, the relationships within the model indicate what can happen and so have a predictive value. A watch is a method of transforming time—an abstract concept, into the position of one piece of metal relative to another; a book is a transformation of ideas into black and white patterns of more or less permanence; money is the transformation of work into pieces of paper. Lastly we have mathematics the most ambitious model building system in the universe of knowledge. There is a paradox here in the traditional concepts as the square root of negative numbers, incommensurables, and other idealized constructs that have no counterpart in physical reality. The continual testing of models is a fundamental part of the methodology of any discipline with a scientific bias, either real or imaginary. The social scientist uses biological models to help him in measuring the phenomena of social change; indeed it is often an index to the prestige of a discipline to assess the way in which its models and techniques are used by other disciplines.

Physics provided the main paradigm in the nineteenth century and still influences the field of social psychology. A case in point is the work of Kurt Lewin (35) who, influenced by the thinking of the physical sciences, conceives of psychological behaviour as events occuring in a kind of space like that of the physical sciences. Hence we have psychic space, social space, semantic space—terms which have become part of the vocabulary of the sociologist and psychologist in describing physical behaviour. One of the more frequently used mental models (indeed so familiar that it escapes our notice) is the metaphor. To appreciate the intellectual or scientific

16

function of metaphors we need only pick out a page or two in any philosophical or scientific treatise.

The importance of this point will be borne in on us when we reflect how many of the passages, which at first sight we take for literal truths, are, in fact, metaphors to which we have grown accustomed. We come across such dead metaphors as 'the root of the problem', 'the progress of thought', 'the flow of electricity'; indeed, whenever we speak of the mind doing anything, collecting its data, perceiving the external world and the like, we are using the metaphor of *reification*, just as we use the metaphor of personification when we speak of bodies attracting or repelling each other.

1.4 THE USES OF MODELS IN COMMUNICATION

Every communication situation differs in some way from another; therefore, in order to make any general statement about the communication process, we have to isolate certain elements that all communication situations have in common and it is these components and their interrelationships that we have to consider in constructing a general model. One of the most cogent arguments for the methodological use of models is put forward by a neuro-physiologist working in a field which has a direct bearing upon the psychology of communication:

Where there are few facts and many impossible connections the subject may be understood without much difficulty; but where there are many facts from diverse sources and nothing can be assumed impossible special tactics must be used to enable the ordinary mind to see the wood rather than the trees. Perhaps the simplest and most agreeable device in such a situation is to construct models in order to reproduce the main features of the system under observation (36).

Within the field of communication, a model consists of what Kenneth Sereno (37) calls 'an idealized description necessary for an act of communication to occur'. This model replicates in abstract terms the essential features of the process and eliminates what it deems to be the unnecessary details of communication in the real world. Models differ widely in the way they represent the process of human communication. Those models which are mathematical, describe the communication process as analogous to the operations of an information processing machine and may be compared with what Floyd Matson (38) and Ashley Montagu call the linear or '*monologic*' definition of communication. Though, as we shall see,

17

the use of models in communication theory is mainly a post-war phenomenon. Aristotle (39), in his treatise on rhetoric, puts forward the first basic analysis of the communication process in the three necessary components: 'the speaker', 'the speech' and 'the audience'. Each of these is necessary to the communication act and we can organize our study of the process under the headings: 1 the person who speaks, 2 the speech he produces and 3 the person who listens.

One of the most frequently cited contemporary models and, perhaps, one of the most influential, is the one put forward by Claude Shannon (40) and later developed by Warren Weaver in their classic work which is regarded as a milestone in the history of communication theory. For Shannon and Weaver the ingredients of the communication system are:

SOURCE—TRANSMITTER—SIGNAL—
RECEIVER—DESTINATION

It must be emphasized at the outset that both men were mainly interested in the problems of telecommunications *not* in the human communication system as such; but if we translate the source into the speaker, the signal into the speech, and the destination into the listener we have the Aristotelian model plus two additional components: a transmitter which sends the message and a receiver which catches the message. The former corresponds to the voice production of the speaker and the latter with the eardrum of the listener. So the communication system may be described as:

INFORMATION SOURCE—TRANSMITTER—
CHANNEL—DESTINATION

The enemy of this system is *noise* which, in Shannon's terms, were usually the problems of electric current or anything which interfered with the fidelity of the message transmission.

If we transfer this model to the library situation, we find that a human being (the source) may type a message consisting of letters and spaces on the keyboard of a teletypewriter. The teletypewriter serves as a transmitter that encodes each character as a sequence of electrical impulses, which may be on or off current, or no current. The electrical impulses are transmitted by a pair of wires to another typewriter which acts as a receiver and prints out the letters and spaces. These in turn are read by the library assistant who acts as a message destination. If there is any extraneous current this may interfere with the accuracy of the transmission. This, then, is the

18

concept of *noise*. Other examples of noise are: static on a radio set, badly produced or smudged typography on catalogue cards which often may affect the retrieval of a document from the system. An extension of the concept of physical noise is *semantic noise*, which may appear in human intercourse as a faulty syntax or ill-chosen terms which the receiver cannot decode or recognise. (D K Berlo (41), a prominent communication scientist, has simplified the Shannon-Weaver model as:

SOURCE—MESSAGE—CHANNEL—RECEIVER

and it is this model which provides a framework for the following chapters. To explicate this process further, we can say that all communication has some *source*—some person or group of persons with a *purpose* in engaging in communication. Let us, then, accept as given, that the source has *ideas, needs, intentions, information* and *purpose*. The purpose of the communicator has to be expressed in terms of the message which has to be translated into a *code*: a systematic set of symbols (language or a surrogate) in order to convey the concepts in his head to the head of the receiver. In interpersonal communication this *encoding* function is performed by the vocal mechanisms of the source producing words, cries, or musical notes, or the muscular systems which produce writing or gestures. The next component needed is the *channel*. Although communication theory has devised more refined and sophisticated definitions of channel, for our purpose we can think of it as a medium or a carrier of messages. The source may have a choice of channels—he may decide to write (using print and paper as channel), use the telephone (electrical impulses), or shout (using the airwaves as a channel).

We have so far a communication source, an encoding mechanism, a message, and channel, but there is still something missing— communication has not taken place as yet. There is an old question attributed to the Buddhist sage: 'What is the sound of a tree falling in the forest?' The answer is, no sound but sound waves if there is no human ear to decode, or as R Bridgman the physicist puts it, sound waves if you are a physicist; sounds if you are a psychologist. When we talk, someone must listen; when we write, someone must read; *communication is a social act*. An adaptation of the Shannon Weaver model to a library situation produces the following components of the communication system. Reader, Mr A is a communication source, he has a purpose or need in producing a message. His central nervous system orders his speech mechanism to construct a message to explain his purpose and the speech mechanism acts as an encoder producing the message; 'May I see a copy of yesterday's *Times*?' The message is transmitted by sound waves (the channel) so that assistant Miss B can receive it. Miss B's hearing mechanism decodes the message into nervous impulses, sending them to the nervous system which responds with the message and complies (hopefully) with the request.

At a further remove the reader Mr A may engage in communication with the writer of *The times* editorial; the basic difference is that now there is a *medium* interposed between them. The message includes the words on the page and the way the words are arranged (syntax); the message is transmitted to him through the medium of the newspaper by means of light waves; his eye is the decoder, retranslating the type into nervous impulses and sending them to the brain. He may respond by hurrying home to write an irate letter to the editor on some issue which has upset him.

A wider social context is assumed by Harold Lasswell (42) in his famous formula of the five 'W's': *Who* is saying *What* to *Whom* through *Which Channel* and with *What Effect*. These models can be as a framework for discussing the flow of information within society. For example, if we use Berlo's model, we get the following structure:

SOURCE	MESSAGE	CHANNEL	RECEIVER
Press	Words		General
Publishing	Mathematical	Print	audiences.
Research	symbols.	Electronic	Specialized
Organizations.	Pictorial	Media	audiences.
Governments,	images.		

Churches and other social organizations,
Television; Radio and
publishing.

Or using the Lasswellian model:

WHO	Communicating organisations, their natures and functions.
WHAT	The nature of the content: informative, entertaining, educative.
WHOM	The nature and receptivity of the audience.
CHANNEL	Print media, audio-visual media, automatic data processing.
EFFECT	The nature of the effect or response of the audience. The ways in which it *affects* the communicator,

20

thus moving the problem back full circle.

At any point in time there is always someone attempting to communicate with someone else, whether these are groups or individuals. This raises some interesting questions for the librarian. The author is a communicator who wishes to say something to an audience. He chooses his medium, it may be a book or journal article, an audio-tape or a visual signal which acts as a channel. Does the library act as a secondary channel? Would the audience be impeded in receiving the message if libraries did not exist? Is the library purely a passive channel? Or does it act in a more active sense as an agency?—a concept much favoured by Jesse Shera (43).

1.5 INFORMATION THEORY AND INFORMATION
Much of the earlier work on communication systems tended to describe the communication process as linear in nature, that is, communication was depicted much in the manner of a conveyor belt; as a one way transmission of messages to a final destination. However, one important concept which did emerge was that of information theory, or in American usage, communication theory. It is generally accepted that information theory dates back to Shannon's classic work, but according to J R Peirce (44), its roots stretch back further into the field of statistical mechanics and physics.

One has to be clear at the outset that information theory is not a theory of information in the same sense that the term is used by the social scientist or the librarian; although there are many important comparisons which may be used, both to clarify the human communication process and the social function of librarianship. Information theory, as Colin Cherry (45) remarks, might well be called a theory of 'signal transmission'. It has an extremely sophisticated mathematical base, concerned chiefly with entropy or the uncertainty of the sequences of related events in a system. To the communication engineer it is a measure of the commodity he is trying to transmit, and that measure of uncertainty or choice is called a 'bit'. This term, which is a contraction of binary digit, is the measure of uncertainty between 'yes or no'; 'heads and tails' when both are equally likely, or the classic choice we exercise when choosing left or right unpredictably, when both are equally likely. The symbols 0 and 1 can easily specify yes or no, heads or tails, left or right.

Shannon showed, in principle, how to measure the information rate of a message source, whether it be a person speaking or writing, or the output of a television camera, in terms of bits per message. But what must be emphasised is that the communication engineer is not concerned with *meaning*, he is concerned with *channel capacity*. In fact, Cherry makes this point abundantly clear, that the object is fidelity of transmission and it matters not whether the channel transmits highly important information of national importance or the sordid details of the most trivial gossip. Meaning belongs to the realm of the behavioural sciences and, as yet, is beyond mathematical quantification. The difficulty has been put thus in a little jingle:

Shannon and Wiener and I
Have found it confusing to try
To measure sagacity and human capacity
In Sigma$_i$ P$_i$, log P$_i$.

The last expression being the basic formula for observed entropy.

In the broad sense, however, information is any content that reduces uncertainty or the number of possibilities in a situation; and on the social and biological plane of human activity, all our behaviour patterns are geared to the reduction of uncertainty. Meaning, though it is interrelated with information, is a difficult concept to define; depending as it does on the response of the individual to the message. An example will illustrate this point. If we picture a waiting room outside a hospital maternity ward. Inside the waiting room 'expectant' fathers wait for information. The nurse comes in and says 'Mr Jones, you have a boy.' This announcement imparts one bit of information to the reast of the people in the room but was *meaning* only for Mr Jones, that is, his own subjective response to this bit of information and its implications for him.

Information in the wider sense is not limited to facts in reference books and documents; although the work of the librarian in exploiting these channels of transmission is reducing uncertainty when he supplies the enquirer with information. Information in the social sense may include emotions, facts and opinions, guidance and persuasion. Social behaviour tends towards uncertainty reduction. When we say 'Good morning' to someone, in this instance, we are not necessarily making a statement of meteorological fact; we are

22

giving him information on our disposition towards him, or establishing what has been called 'phatic communion'.

The ancient idea of transferring a box of facts from one mind to another is no longer a satisfactory way of thinking about human communication; each person comes to a given piece of information influenced by his own needs, ideas and preconceptions. In the broad biological sense information is any content which helps the organism to structure the environment in which it acts. For instance, the organism will *classify* its environment into 'eatable and non-eatable' or 'dangerous and not dangerous'; a binary method which enables it to survive. Before we investigate whether or not the communications engineer has anything to offer us, we shall look at the term 'system', since we have been talking so much about communication 'systems'.

A system, according to Wilbur Schramm, 'is any part of an information chain which is capable of existing in one or more states, or in which one or more events can occur' (46). Examples within our own everyday experience are telegraph wires, the vibrating metal diaphragm of a microphone, pulsating sound waves, the basilar membrane of the ear, and the optic nerve. Each of these is capable of assuming *different states* and each can be coupled to other systems to form a communication *chain*. In this sense, a library is a coupling system bringing the author's work before the eye of the reader, or acting as a link between one research worker and another. If information is to be transferred, the systems must obviously be coupled; as, for example, when light frequencies strike the eye and cause discharges in the optic nerve, these systems are coupled. A break in the coupling will prevent any information from being transferred; in much the same way as when a student's attention wanders in class he misses the substance of the discussion.

Most human communication chains contain a large number of coupled systems. This can be seen in the many coupling systems, from the first encoding of the author's message, its diffusion through the publisher's network to the bookseller, and again throughout the accessions system to the library shelves. If any break occurs in the system, information has not been transmitted. We can now say what communication means to the communication theorist. 'Communication occurs when two corresponding systems, coupled together through one or more non-corresponding systems, assume identical states as a result of signal transfer along the chain' (47). Unless the sound that goes into the telephone is reproduced by the sound that comes out of the telephone at the other end of the line, we do not have communication.

In mass communications the chains of coupled systems take on quite remarkable characteristics: they are often very long; the account of a news event in South America must pass through a long communication chain before it reaches its destination. As we shall see later, the mass media themselves are networks of systems coupled in such a way as to decode events in the environment, interpreting, storing and encoding in much the same way that we associate with human communicators. The librarian is also concerned with information science and, of course, information technology; the study of the information seeking behaviour of enquirers, how their questions are framed, and the influence of information on their behaviour. This is still a field of enquiry and endeavour which is in search of a definition. The term 'informatics' has been proposed as 'the systematic study of information transfer'. There is another school of thought which puts forward information science as a social science, since it ultimately deals with human behaviour. When the work of Shannon and Weaver was published, hopes were raised that the Shannon theory would be applicable to human communication in general; and for some years linguists, psychologists and others searched hopefully for this wider measure of information which could also embrace meaning and human interest. No such measure has yet been found.

We do not know enough yet about the memories and motivation of human beings to be able to measure their interest in information, or the effect of information upon their behaviour. Unlike the machine, the human being is sensitive to the context in which he operates and is often burdened by conflicting needs. Unlike the channel of the communications engineer, he is not indifferent to the nature of the input nor indeed of the output. The principal uses of these models of communication is to structure our thinking, and help us to frame questions regarding our own professional skills as well as helping us to examine the mass media as information systems.

1.6 REDUNDANCY

Two further concepts which emerged from the original speculations of communication theorists were *redundancy* and *entropy*: two interrelated concepts essential to the understanding of the communications process. All threats to the efficiency of a

24

communication system are diminished in some measure by the redundancy employed in the process. It is, in fact, a special counteraction against noise: the message is repeated and summarised just to make sure it reaches the destination. In response to various obstacles of a psychological origin in man, nature has seemingly made provision for redundancy. It is a standard device in rhetoric, one example is 'litotes', which is the expression of an affirmative by the negative of its contrary. This is how St Paul gave emphasis in the statement that he was 'a citizen of no mean city'; or, at a slighly less exalted level there is the use of incremental repetition in ballads. Linguists have calculated that the English language has about fifty per cent redundancy, which enables us to compile crosswords. Redundancy would seem to be one of nature's safeguards both in the biological and in the cosmic sense, the spirit of which is so admirably captured by George Bernard Shaw (48):

The great life force has hit upon the idea of the clockworker's pendulum, using the earth as its bob; the history of each oscillation which seems so novel to us the actors, is but the history of the last oscillation repeated.

It is an interesting point that this redundancy does give us some confidence in the human framework. Indeed, most of the communications made by a man are mostly redundant and could be a possible reason for the current fear of machines; perhaps they are a subconscious recognition of a fear that a computerised society would be unnatural, because it eliminates our natural proclivity for redundancy. As George Gordon (49) asks:

How might we feel if we were exposed to a fumbling computer mechanism with fifty per cent redundancy built into it? Might we regard it as being more natural than its highly efficient brother.

Marshall McLuhan, in discussing the cybernetic superiority of speech as compared with writing, uses his own term 'hot' as a slangy gloss on the communication engineer's concept of redundancy, or the fact that messages carry more information than is strictly needed to get their information across. Once speech is committed to writing, the receiver has to do more work in inferring what is meant: 'reading between the lines' as it were, and the danger of ambiguity is much greater.

1.7 CYBERNETICS AND INFORMATION

Two years after Shannon and Weaver's work was published, there emerged a work no less epoch making in its impact on communication and on the whole realm of human knowledge: this was the classic work of Norbert Wiener(50). Linear models, though adequate in elucidating certain problems, overlooked one significant dimension: the sender monitors each segment of the message which he transmits, and this may influence the sending of further messages. This consideration became the basis of the cybernetic model of the communication process. Norbert Wiener's name is usually associated with the founding of the science of cybernetics but its origins are much older, finding its basic ideas in the work of Walter Rosenblueth (51), W Ross Ashby (52) and others. The cybernetic model of Wiener is based on adaptive information which it interprets before doing something as a consequence. In the linear model, the rifleman aims at a stationary target; in the cybernetic model, the target may move in any direction after the rifleman has fired his bullet and in order to hit it he must have a cybernetic system of communicating. That is, he must adjust his aim on the basis of the information received by his eye.

The second world war highlighted this need for research into cybernetics because, for the first time in the history of warfare, missiles, rockets and planes were approaching the speed of sound and there was the problem of rangefinding for anti-aircraft guns in high-speed warfare. Speed and accuracy were essential in the tracking of objects. To meet this need, machines were programmed in such a way that they could make decisions and instruct various parts of the anti-aircraft guns to operate on the basis of these decisions; machines were now 'thinking' and 'communicating'. The important point is that these machines were not automatic in the sense that a see-saw is automatic; they employed a mechanism know as *feedback*. A common example of this phenomenon is the adaptive mechanism of the body as it adjusts to changes in the environment through what is called 'homeostatic control'. J O Wisdom (53) puts the central core of cybernetic thought thus:

The basic hypothesis of cybernetics is that the chief mechanism is one of negative feedback, but the field of study is not limited to feedback of a negative kind. Cybernetics makes the hypothesis that the negative feedback explains behaviour as 'purposive and adaptive behaviour'.

In fact it raises a metaphysical point as to whether there is teleological or purposive behaviour even in the inanimate forms of reality. Wiener's work concentrates upon two central concepts;

communication and control, emphasizing the implications for information and entropy:

When I give an order to a machine the situation is not essentially different from that which arises when I give an order to a person. In other words as far as my consciousness goes I am aware that an order has gone out and that a signal of compliance has come back. To me personally the fact that a signal in its intermediate stages has gone through a machine rather than through a person is irrelevant and does not alter my relation to the signal. Thus the theory of control whether human, animal or mechanical is a chapter in the theory of messages (54).

This is the charter for man-machine interface, but it by no means is a substitute for interpersonal communication: it is the transmission of a command, not a communication between equals. The machine, at least at present, is oblivious to the social context, to the nuances of the situation, to the status of the communicator; nor can it have any specific attitude to the message. Information transfer, though it may resemble interpersonal communication in some instances, is by no means a co-terminous concept. The concept of control, however, was to have a deep and lasting influence upon the sociology of communication and probably gave rise to the many pessimistic premonitions which permeate Wiener's work. The commands through which we exercise control over our environment are a *kind of information* we impart to it. Man is immersed in a world which he perceives through his sense organs. His sensory input is co-ordinated through the brain and nervous system until, after the proper process of storage and collation, it is combined with his already accumulated store of information to influence further action.

One of the fruits of this intersection of psychology and communication theory is this psychological conception of man as an information gathering, information processing system. Although it is a very cold and rational ideal of man, it is useful in determining the social function of the library and, indeed, in analysing society itself as an information receiving and processing system. The library receives, decodes and imposes order on the information it gets from its environment; it imposes order upon chaos. The human organism also receives information from, and imposes order on, its environment. Information and order are therefore closely related; and the enemy of this activity is called 'entropy'.

The term 'entropy' is usually strange to students of social communication, which is small wonder since it was originally borrowed from physics where it is enshrined in the second law of thermodynamics. Now entropy (transformed energy) is the name for degraded energy which has been dissipated by friction and other wasteful process into the random motion of molecules, and which cannot be retrieved. In the wider sense it has been expanded to denote the measure of disorder in a system: a usage strongly deprecated by Colin Cherry (55). The implications then are, that in a closed system, entropy always tends towards a maximum: eventually the system must unwind itself from cosmos to chaos. All living systems, however, are 'open systems', that is to say they maintain their complex forms and functions through the exchange of energy and information with their environments. So, instead of running down like a mechanical clock that dissipates its energies through friction, the living organism constantly builds up more complex forms of energy from the environment it feeds on; building up more complex patterns of information from its sensory input.

As distinct from a structural system, organisms are *functional* systems: that is they learn. This new approach to information was largely the result of a conflict between physics and biology to provide a definitive paradigm for man. The idea that organisms were active, instead of being passively at the mercy of their environment, owes much to the work of Ludwig von Bertalanffy (56) and is an influential contribution to the sociology of information. For the librarian there is the salutary thought that a library is, or should be, an open system continually engaged in an information exchange with its environment. Ranganathan was probably thinking of this when he enunciated the law that the 'library is a growing organism'

In communication theory we consider a message source—such as a writer or speaker who may produce on a given occasion one of many possible messages. The amount of information conveyed by the message increases as the amount of uncertainty as to what the message actually will be becomes greater: or, as J R Peirce puts it:

A message which is one out of ten possible messages conveys a smaller amount of information than a message which is one out of a million possible messages. The entropy of communication then is a measure of this uncertainty, and the uncertainty or entropy is taken as a measure of the information conveyed by the message (58).

In other words, the more we know about what message the source will produce, the less the uncertainty and the less the information: the glib cliches produced by politicians, indulging in a predictable posture to a crisis situation, give less information than the newly-minted thought of the original thinker. Entropy is the great enemy of information and redundancy and, in Shannon's terms, redundancy is one of the safeguards built into a system to combat it. In this terminology 'negative entropy' becomes a way of referring to the power of life to build up complex systems out of simpler elements; to fashion order out of disorder, and to impose structure upon the chaotic and the amorphous.

It is significant that Weiner defined information as essentially a 'negative entropy' and devoted some considerable space in his seminal work (59) in speculating whether entropy may not be the Manichean devil, who by bluff and deceit actively creates disorder; or the devil of St Augustine, who connotes absence of order or incompleteness. Entropy now has a metaphysical status and librarians whose *raison d'etre* is the imposition of order, or negative entropy, might well be tempted to subscribe to the Manichean, active chaos-creating principle, continually frustrating his attempts to impose order and organization. Life, according to Wiener, only exists because there are limited enclaves within the cosmos whose direction seems opposed to the universal tendency towards disorder, and in which there is a limited tendency toward organization; but it is a very fragile balance.

The lesson for the sociologist of information is, that the more complex the society, the greater the demand on the information processing systems and channels; and society is obliged to meet this need or give way to chaos and entropy. To compound this problem, social structures tend to become more complex, as if in response to some evolutionary law; and as this happens, their information-bearing systems grow with what they feed on. This has always seemed to be the librarian's dilemma—satisfaction of information needs stimulates an even greater demand, which places a correspondingly greater strain on the system; the more successful he is, the nearer he is to destroying his own system.

As Schrodinger (6o) puts it: 'what an organism feeds on is negative entropy' or, in our case, information. Society in this sense is an information-seeking organism and the library as an active part of the nervous system must experience a correlative rate of growth, and more important still, maintain contact with the other networks within the social system. If it does not, society must go the way of the dinosaur whose body we are told grew overmuch in relation to his brain. J Ziman (61) had this analogy in mind when dealing with the problems of organizations, he said: *'A research organization without a library is like a decorticated car, the motor organization continues to function but lacks co-ordination or purpose.'*

1.71 ENTROPY, REDUNDANCY AND THE LIBRARIAN

The term entropy will probably be strange to most students, unless they have specialised in physics, but redundancy will probably be more familiar. The strange thing is that we were often rebuked at school for tautologies; but in fact redundancy is used in communication as a safeguard against entropy or noise. Redundancy is a measure of certainty or predictability and in communication theory the more redundant a system the less information it carries in a given time. This is true also of social communication. We use ritual redundancies such as 'actually' and 'Good morning' or 'Would you like to shelve this trolley of books' as a disguised order; such a procedure acts as a social lubricant and pays some homage to the status and dignity of the person. But the paradoxical point is that any language or code without redundancy would be chaos; sometimes we increase redundancy to make sure the message gets across.

The English language displays a great deal of redundancy — about fifty percent according to the communication engineers. We have some probabilities that some letters will follow others; if a 'q' occurs on a teletype line followed by two obvious errors the operator can be sure that the 'q' is followed by 'u' and then by another vowel. We encounter the redundancy of the English language when we compile an understandable telegram and, as librarians, when we compile an index. The problem for the librarian, as for any communicator, is how much redundancy may be used to avoid ambiguity yet without swamping the message. The most economcal writing is not always the most efficient; the more abbreviated the message the greater the danger of ambiguity, indeed, the folklore of librarianship is rich in howlers on the mis-interpretation of index languages. Like any communication act much will depend upon what the reader brings to the message. A librarian may choose to explain the function of a catalogue in fifty words which would be a redundancy highly unnecessary for another librarian, but vital for a layman. In the library situation the librarian may act as a necessary redundancy factor in elucidating the index for the baffled reader, bringing the formal system of the index into contact with the concept system of the user.

Entropy is the tendency towards disorganization in a system and most people will have little difficulty in recounting personal experiences of their battles against entropy. It is the continual and ever present danger in a communication system. The longer the channel of communication, the greater the opportunity for this demon to achieve his objective; as the astounded military commander of the first world war found when he received an urgent request to 'send three and fourpence' for someone who was 'going to a dance'. Whether the reinforcements did arrive, and the advance made, we do not know. A collection of unsorted books is in a state of maximum entropy and the librarian imposes information and order in the form of a classification system. It is noteworthy that the place were entropy often strikes is in the cataloguing and accessions department, where material is more easily lost before it is placed within the framework of order in the form of a classification scheme.

Information then is really the reduction of uncertainty, and is the opposite of entropy; in fact, information is sometimes called 'negative entropy'. If we know that a train is due to depart from 'somewhere, somewhen', the situation is highly random and entropic; there are infinite possibilities. But, if we find that it departs from a station in Wales, then the entropy is reduced and we have received valuable information. If we find it is from Aberystwyth, then the uncertainty is further reduced. Then we find the day of departure, the time and the platform number, and there is a gradual attainment of certainty and order. Information, entropy, redundancy and feedback are very important terms in communication theory. They are also essential in understanding the principles of cybernetics, which is the study of how open systems exchange information with their environment and deals with the comparison of control and communication in men and machines. It is vitally important for two reasons: it shows us what men have in common with the machines they create and how man himself thinks, reacts, behaves and learns. The term cybernetics is derived from the Greek 'kybernetes', meaning a steersman; and one of the reasons for choosing the term was that the steering mechanism of a ship was a good example of a feedback mechanism. We can also see the feedback mechanism at work when we ride a bicycle; as the bicycle veers to the left we correct the turn by turning the handlebars to the right and so on. The ordinary household thermostat is another example; if the temperature goes down, information reaches the thermostat that the room is too cold (this is called the input) and the thermostat then consults its instructions which may be 'if the temperature falls below 70 degrees start the furnace'.

Society monitors its environment in much the same way, adjusting to changes or crisis situations. However, this calls for communication channels to relay the information, and in contemporary society the mass media of communications do just this: they survey the environment and help in decision-making, acting rather like a watcher on the hillside. The public library acts as the social memory, carrying the transcript of what has been done in similar situations or crises in the past. But it also acts as a cybernetic system, reacting to changes in the environment. For example, changes in the audience structure, or the entry of new ethnic groups, will influence its book selection and the building of new industries may make it readjust its ideas about its information services.

1.8 SOCIAL RELEVANCE OF CYBERNETICS

The three main pillars of the cybernetic approach to communication are first: a probabilistic view of the world; secondly an interest in feedback cycles and processes; thirdly an interest in information processing in self-steering mechanisms and their capabilities. As a communication model, it is particularly important for the librarian, the information specialist and also for the teacher in librarianship and information sciences. It provides the teacher with a framework for explaining the social problems of information processing; how society functions as an information system; the function of the library within the social process; and the problems of man-machine interface.

Within the terms of the traditional linear model, the librarian has usually been the passive receiver of requests and demands, and he has not infrequently compensated for this by overwhelming the enquirer with 'noise', in the communication sense of the term. In the cybernetic model he is a listener and a programmer, an active partner in an enquiry situation. He has been traditionally conditioned to the idea that his services are linear in essence. Now the model can shift from a preoccupation with message design, to the creation of situations where the librarian and enquirer can interact as systems; each adjusting to the other and interpreting and interrogating the information system in a co-operative enterprise.

On the wider social scale, the conceptual model of cybernetics represents the most influential theory of communication to arise in our century and it is having an influence on almost every field of knowledge. It has, for example, been applied to the problems of politics and the interpretation of history by Kark Deutsch (2); and its influence upon management theory has been pervasive and far reaching, an influence that has also reached librarianship(63). There are also the more fascinating and sensational products which afford much delight to the more pretentious forms of journalism: stories of artificial tortoises who find and connect themselves to sources of power when their batteries run low; electric hands which can follow instructions and locate an object, pick it up, and put it in a certain place; a 'perceptron', which is teaching itself to read; and the inevitable computer which attempts to rival the poetic graces of John Milton.

Even taking into account the naive comparisons of the uncritical, our modern communications systems are greatly indebted to this 'second industrial revolution' as it has been called, and to quote Floyd Matson (64), 'if mechanical power was the master metaphor or paradigm of the first industrial revolution, communication and control provide the characteristic model of our time'. To the sociologist the concept of social control strikes rather a chilly note, and Wiener himself was fully aware of this danger. Control is necessarily directive and manipulative: all communication tends to be conducted in the imperative mood. We transmit order to machines but we do not, as yet, debate propositions with them. There is always a dangerous analogy for the potential dictator over-influenced by the ideal of the machine as a model of social efficiency. This kind of communication is what Buber (65) would call 'monologic' as opposed to 'dialogic' theory; the monologic system creates a society where communication is fashioned to ensure compliance rather than achieve understanding — this is the real fear of social cybernetics.

There is, however, a relevant corrective in the work of Anatol Rapoport. (66) He is deeply concerned with the mathematical contructs of game theory, particularly as it is cultivated by decision makers. Mankind tends to be divided, not ethnically, racially or geographically but intellectually and psychologically. On one side, says Rapoport, are the exponents of strategic gamesmanship who espouse the monologic form of communication and base their strategy on the theory of control: these are the men who regard politics as the continuation of war by other means. On the other side are the dialogue men, who believe in politics as the art of reaching consensus and the final end as the achievement of understanding. In any conflict between them the question in the mind of the strategist is, 'In a conflict how best may I gain an advantage over him?' Thomas Hobbes, the English political philosopher, drew a picture of man as egocentric and self-seeking; a view which has influenced what some sociologists call a 'conflict model' of society. The kind of communication just mentioned exemplifies this rather pessimistic view of human nature. The 'dialogic man' however, asks himself: 'If I gain an advantage over my opponent, what kind of man will I become?' There would seem to by many ways of viewing man: as a moral being, a social being, thinker and worker; all of which give rise to major fields of knowledge.

Before we proceed to the next chapter we must deal with the almost inevitable duplication of the terms 'knowledge' and 'information'. The task of defining knowledge lies mainly within the province of the philosopher and, as we can see, the term is used in many senses in ordinary speech. There is the old crone bending over her cauldron and muttering mysteriously: 'I know what I know' or we may examine the many meanings of the statement: 'I know that my Redeemer liveth', which could be taken as statement of belief. Or again 'I know the Prime Minister' or 'I know the road to London': statements which imply a different sense of 'knowing'. Many writers insist on distinguishing 'information' from knowledge by having information refer to the process or act by which knowledge is transmitted; that is signals, signs or messages. Others use the term 'information' to refer to disconnected facts or events or 'patterns of stimuli' and confine the term knowledge to a systematic and ordered system; for example, personal knowledge. It is in this sense that the term will be used here, although one recognises the difficulty of drawing a logical division between them.

1 Aristotle *The rhetoric.*
2 Franklin D Knower 'The present state of experimental speech, communication research' *in* Paul Reid ed: *Frontiers of speech communication research* New York, Holt, 1957.
3 Erwin Bettinghaus *Message preparation; the nature of proof* New York,

Bobbs-Merrill, 1966.

4 Karl Jaspers *Man in the modern age* New York, Doubleday, 1957,

5 Martin Buber *Between man and man* London, MacMillan, 1965.

6 Paul Tillich *Theology of culture* London, Oxford University Press, 1965.

7 Joost Meerloo *Conversation and communication* New York, International Universities Press, 1971.

8 Edward T Hall *Silent language* New York, Doubleday, 1959.

9 Muzafer Sherif *Social psychology* rev. ed, New York, Harper, 1959.

10 Wilbur Schramm *Process and effects of communication* 2nd ed, Urbana, University of Illinois Press, 1971.

11 A J Ayer *The problems of knowledge* Harmondsworth (Middx), Penguin Books, 1966.

12 Benjamin Lee Whorf *Language, thought and reality* Cambridge (Mass), MII Press, 1956.

13 Noam Chomsky *Language and mind* New York, Harcout Brace and World, 1967. Also his attack on the behaviourist position in his classic review of B F Skinner's *Verbal behaviour* (in *Language*, 35, 1959).

14 Claude Shannon *and* Warren Weaver *The mathematical theory of communication* Urbana, University of Illinois Press, 1949.

15 Ludwig von Bertalanffy *General systems theory* London Allen Lane, 1967.

16 I A Richards *Principles of literary criticism* London, Routledge, 1929.

17 F R Leavis *New bearings in English poetry* London, Chatto and Windus, 1933.

18 Harvey Cox *The secular city* New York, MacMillan, 1966.

19 Richard Meier *Communications theory and urban growth* Harvard, MIT Press, 1962

20 T R Nilson 'On defining communication' *Speech teacher* 6, 1957 10-17.

21 Floyd Mateson *and* Ashley Montague *The human dialogue* New York, Free Press, 1967.

22 T R Nilson *Op cit.*

23 Theodore Newcomb *Social psychology* New York, Holt, Rinehart and Wilson, 1955 p 269.

24 Wilbur Schramm *Process of mass communication* 2nd ed, Urbana, University of Illinois Press, 1970 p 24.

25 S S Stevens 'Introduction: A definition of communication' *The journal of the Acoustical Society of America* 22 November 1950, p 689.

26 Claude E Shannon *and* Warren Weaver *The mathematical theory of communication* Urabana, University of Illinois Press, 1949, p 3.

27 Charles Morris *Signs, language and behaviour* New York, Prentice Hall, 1946, p 118.

28 George Lundberg *Foundations of sociology* New York, MacMillan, 1939, p 253.

29 Charles Cooley *Social organization; a study of the larger mind* New York, Scribner, 1924, p 61.

30 Edward Sapir Article on 'Communication' in *Encyclopaedia of the social sciences* New York, Mac Millan, 1930-35.

31 Discussed in Teodor Shanin ed *The rules of the game: cross disciplinary essays on models in modern scholarly thought* London, Tavistock Publications, 1972.

32 Kenneth Boulding *The image: essays in the sociology of knowledge* Ann Arbor, Michigan University Press, 1956.

33 Thomas S Kuhn *The structure of scientific revolutions* Chicago, University of Chicago Press, 1962.

34 Edward de Bono *Use of lateral thinking* London, Cape, 1967.

35 Kurt Lewin *Field of theory in the social sciences* London, Tavistock Publications, 1963.

36 Walter Grey *in* E H Adrian ed *Brain mechanisms and consciousness* Oxford, Blackwell, 1954.

37 Kenneth Sereno *and* D Mortensen *Foundations of communication theory* New York, Harper, 1970.

38 Floyd Matson *and* Ashley Montagu *The human dialogue: perceptives on communication* New York, Free Press, 1967.

39 Aristotle *The rhetoric* ed W D Ross, London, Oxford University Press, 1945, vol xi, p 14.

40 Claude C Shannon *and* Warren Weaver *The mathematical theory of communication* Urbana, University of Illinois Press, 1949.

41 D K Berlo *The Process of communication* New York, Holt, Rinehart and Winston, 1960.

42 Harold Lasswell 'Structure and function of communication in society' *in* L Bryson *Communication of ideas*, 1948.

43 Jesse Shera 'The library as a social agency' *Journal of documentation* December 1955, P 413–5.

44 John R Pierce *Symbols, signals and noise* London, Hutchinson, 1966.

45 Colin Cherry *Human communication* 2nd ed, Cambridge (Mass) MIT Press, 1969.

46 Wilbur Schramm 'Information theory and mass communication' *Journalism quarterly* Spring 1955, p 131-46.

47 *Ibid*

48 G B Shaw *Man and superman* London, Constable.

49 George Gordon *The language of communication: a logical and psychological examination* New York, Hastings House, 1969, p 36.

50 Norbet Wiener *Cybernetics or control and communication in the animal and the machine* Harvard, MIT Press, 1948.

51 W Rosenblueth *Autonomic neuroeffector systems* London, MacMillan, 1937.

52 W Ross Ashby 'Adaptiveness and equilibrium' *Journal of mental science* 85, 1940, p 478-83. Also in his book *Design for a brain* New York, Wiley, 1952.

53 J O Wisdom 'The hypothesis of cybernetics' *British journal for the philosophy of science* 37 May 1951, p 1-23.

54 Norbert Wiener *The human use of human beings: cybernetics and society* New York, Houghton Mifflin, 1960 p 25.

55 Colin Cherry *Human communication* 2nd ed Cambridge (Mass), MIT Press, 1970, p 51 and *passim*.

56 Ludwig von Bertalanffy *General systems theory* London, Allen Lane, 1968.

57 Ranganathan *Five laws of library science* Asia Publishing House, 1963.

58 John R Peirce *Symbols, signals and noise* London, Hutchinson, 1962, p 23.

59 Norbert Wiener *Op cit*.

60 Erwin Schrodinger *What is life* Cambridge University Press, 1944, p 72

61 J Z Ziman *Public knowledge: the social dimensions of science* Cambridge University Press, 1969.

62 Karl Deutsch 'Knowledge in the growth of civilization: cybernetics and the history of human thought' *in* Edward Montegomery ed *Foundations of access to knowledge* New York, Syracuse University Press, 1966. Also his

Nerves of government New York, Free Press, 1963.

63 Merrill Flood 'The systems approach to library planning' *Library quarterly* 34 (4) 1964, p 326-8.

64 Floyd Matson *in* Montgomery, *op cit,* p 60.

65 Martin Buber *I and thou* London, Clark, 1962.

66 Anatol Rapoport *Strategy and conscience* New York, Schocken Books, 1969.

67 There is a very readable discussion of this and other models of society *in* Jeremy Boissevain *Friends of friends: networks, manipulators and coalitions* Oxford, Blackwell, 1974.

CHAPTER 2

Communication:
knowledge and culture

THE OBJECTIVES of this chapter are to survey the problems and applicability of communication models to the interpersonal communication situation and to determine the extent to which the social context may influence the idealized models discussed in the last chapter. In surveying and analysing the literature of communication theory, one gets the inescapable impression that the human link in communication is regarded in much the same way as random noise. There is much that is of value in such models as those of Shannon and Weaver, but one feels that once one enters the sphere of social interaction an idealized model serves much the same function as the gold standard does in economic theory—that is, having more of symbolic and reference value rather than serving a utilitarian purpose. Librarianship as a communication science deals with the transmission of information and its ultimate use by human beings; but the main point for the librarian to remember is, that however sophisticated the communications technology may be, there is always a human being at the purposive end. George Miller (1) puts the point thus:

The fact that every communication system winds somewhere home to a human nervous system means that no theory of communication will be complete unless it is capable of treating the system components in a theoretical language so general and so powerful that human beings can be included along with every other component.

There is always the danger that, seduced by the potential of information technology, the human component may be regarded as an unwelcome disturbance in an otherwise well ordered system and should, accordingly, be reduced as much as possible. This temptation is no less dangerous for the librarian who may come to regard himself as a machine minder to whom the human concept system is irrelevant. This stance resembles the attitude of the reductionist-minded communication theorist who, impressed by the inexorable laws of thermodynamics, is forced to admit that noise is inevitable and inescapable; but who believes that, if you are willing to take the trouble, the human elements can be eliminated completely. For many years the concepts of human engineering were phrased in the language of volts, watts and amperes, which have a demonstrably limited value in describing either the vagaries of the human condition or the variables of human behaviour. As long as the human link is distorted to fit an inanimate system, communication theory will make little contribution to the behavioural sciences. Accordingly, within this chapter, I have added to the traditional model the problems of an all-embracing cultural environment—its scope and nature, and its effect on the communication situation. I intend to discuss the nature of the interaction between source and receiver; the cultural factors which bind them together and the nature of the channel, or medium, through which the communication takes place.

Any discussion of man as an information-gathering and an information processing system is bound to stand at the intersection of many specialisms. Chief among the specialists are the philosophers, who will assert that any statements about man inevitably entail statements about knowledge. Then come the empirically minded physiologists, who are concerned with the nervous system of our human *source* and its culminating point the brain. Both disciplines try to answer the rhetorical question of the psalmist: 'What is man thou art mindful of him?'—and will probably agree on very little. Man is a communication system; he receives sensory stimuli from his environment and these raw data are transformed or recorded initially in the sense organs, and subsequently in successive centres of the nervous system. They are transmitted over nerve trunks from one station to another and amplified in the course of transmission. The information is added to and stored for lengthy or short periods to aid decision making. This description, stated baldly, would be simplified and question-begging account of the 'lord of all creation', and would not provide a great deal more information than the average intelligent person might be expected to know. But how does the brain treat this sensory input we are constantly receiving from our environment? J Z Young compares the brain to a gigantic government office or to a calculating machine. This office is an

39

information receiving system. Its efficiency depends upon the co-ordination and networking of its channels of information, and its capacity to decode incoming information. He develops his analogy thus:

The sense organ transmits information to whichever departments of the brain can use it. But how does the brain bring this information together so as to send out the right orders to the bodily territory responsible? Information reaches the brain in a kind of code of impulses passing up the nerve fibres. Information already received is stored in the brain either by sending impulses round closed circuits or in some form corresponding to a print.... Similarly the brain is constantly relating the new impulses that reach it to the information already stored in the tissues (2).

The faculty for information reception and information storage would seem to be a function that man shares with the lowest organism. But in any classroom discussion which compares the brain to a machine, the question will probably arise: 'Man puts the code into the machine, who puts the code into man?' and at once we are over into the realm of the biologist.

There has been a tradition in epistemology started by John Locke (3) (1632-1704), the English philosopher, which considers the mind to be rather like a wax tablet upon which the senses engraved their messages. The implications of this *tabula rasa* theory are that man is a passive creature of his environment and that we learn most if not all of what we do through the acquisition of experience through the senses. In sum, all our experience and knowledge consists of information received through our senses and processed for use. Karl Popper (4) calls this the 'bucket theory of the mind', because it ignores such important factors as the internalising principle which imposes order on this information, and our predispositions to learn, for example, a language. This theory of knowledge was probably a reaction against Plato's theory of forms, which relegated the world of our experiences to an imperfect representation of an ideal world of which we have a glimpse before we are born, or as Wordsworth (5) put it: 'Our birth is but a sleep and a forgetting'.

This theory might account for the internal organising principle in man but, in the eyes of the tough-minded reductionist, it commits the cardinal sin of adducing the invisible to explain the visible. On the other hand to view man as merely a receiver of sensory input

leaves a lot to be explained. The feeling of futility and helplessness engendered by this hypothesis is expressed by A E Housman (6):
'I a stranger and afraid
In a world I never made'
But if the physiologist is correct, experience is not a 'given', in the active sense of the term, and it would therefore seem that the term 'datum' is misleading. We actively impose order upon reality. Instead of being the passive receiver of sense impressions, man creates as he perceives. Sir Russell Brain (7) puts this viewpoint strongly: *'The perceptual world therefore, if I may use the term to describe the whole range of our perceptual experience, in a construct of the percipients brain.'*

The implications for the theory of knowledge and for social communication are far reaching. Reality, then, must to a great extent to be a social construct, created by the collective perceptions of social man. Instead of merely being an extension of matter, man is therefore a product of his culture and his perceptions are conditioned by a common world picture built up by his ancestors. As each baby is born it is bombarded with incoming stimuli and once these stimuli begin to leave their mark on the brain the rules begin to be established; though how these rules get in to the brain we do not as yet know. Young (8) develops the concept of cultural conditioning by speaking of 'the store of rules learnt by years of exploring with the eyes during childhood'. This would seem to accord with the commonsense view that each of us enters the world in a state of nescience. Though the brain is not the *tabula rasa* that Locke thought it was, the basic rules are there to select and encode, and the brain possesses a need for information just as the body needs food. The human brain needs a constant stream of sensory input which is why solitary confinement is such a hard punishment, and the more pernicious interrogation technique of 'hooding' shows how the personality disintegrates when the brain suffers from sensory deprivation.

Together with our biological needs we have the need for information, a need which is both social and psychological. A once favourite topic for speculation by philosophers was the problem of the man born blind, but who regains his sight later in life. The question was, would the new visual reality conform to his internal or imagined construction of it? Would he be overjoyed at the receiving of such a precious gift? This operation has now been performed many times and there is no joy or jubilation: in fact the reverse for he has not been trained in the 'rules' of seeing:

He reports only a mass of spinning colours and lights. He proves to be quite unable to pick out objects by sight to recognise and to name them. He has no conception of space and the objects in it (9).

The implications of this for the communications theorist and the epistemologist is that we do not see things in their pristine integrity, or as things independent of ourselves. We learn from others how to see and there is a substantial literature in educational psychology to support the fact that people from different cultures often see things in a different way. In terms of our model, the source and the receiver may have completely different cultural backgrounds which may cause communication difficulties. Yet if we accept this account of reality based on private experience, there must be an area of private knowledge. If I bump my head on a rock, the pain is my own private experience; the question is then: how does an individual mind reach out to other minds? We have an urge to communicate our experiences; and it is this urge to communicate our private worlds that results in a pooling of private experiences to form a common world picture, or social consensus. Otherwise we become schizophrenic, with each individual carrying around with him his own private view of reality.

We contribute to this 'common pool' and we are indebted to it; and the library is an important agency in this transaction. For instance, I know that there is a place called Greece and I know certain things about it but not on the basis of *direct* sensory experience. It is knowledge which I have inferred from the general world picture; that is, from my reading of the direct perceptions of others. Within our society then there are sources of knowledge which fulfil this communication function. We may say that *The times* is a source of knowledge, or the *Encyclopaedia Britannica*. We may say that certain papers in the *Physical review* are more authoritative about the same problem than either *The times* or *Britannica*. But we could examine this still further and discover that these sources were in turn indebted to other papers, thereby starting an almost infinite regress of indebtedness back to the original eyewitness or experimenter and find that he was still further indebted to someone else.

In general we accept these sources because they form a 'social consensus'; but it is the chief glory of man that he continually

42

questions them and subjects them to scrutiny. The 'library', using the term in the widest frame of reference, not only helps to build this consensus but also acts as a means whereby this consensus may be scrutinized. The library, in both concept and actuality, exists because of the urge of social man to communicate the results of his own private experiences to others; be these experiences the result of rigourous experiments or his own private view of the human condition expressed in the verbal or plastic arts. Michael Polanyi (10) had divided the realm of human knowledge into two domains: public and private, 'Public knowledge' is that which is set out in written form or in maps or mathematical formulae. But, he says, there is another form of knowledge which we have of something we are in the act of doing, although this knowledge is inchoate, unexpressed, and formless. The first kind of knowledge he calls 'explicit' knowledge and the second 'tacit' knowledge. This division would seem to parallel the old division between knowing and understanding as traditonally understood.

Professor Karl Popper (11) gets round this problem of the 'objective' versus 'subjective' world by dividing reality into what he calls the 'three worlds'. World one is the physical world; world two, the world of our conscious experiences; and the world of the logical contents of books and libraries, computer memories and such like, he calls world three. These are three interdependent realms: our consciousness depends upon the physical world and the third world of books and artifacts he regards as an autonomous world which mediates indirect experience. This third world depends upon the interaction between worlds one and two, and the librarian is involved at the nodal point of these many interrelationships. When we compare what we have learned from *direct* experience with what we have learned from *indirect* experience, the scope of our direct knowledge seems startlingly limited. Without the necessary communication links, we are cut off from this third world of Professor Popper's and, if we are cut off from other human beings also, then we are necessarily limited to our own direct experience.

Communication, as well as satisfying the urge within us, makes it possible for us to draw upon the nervous systems of others and learn what our own nervous systems may have missed. Indeed it is this phenomenon which makes society resemble an intricate, co-operative nervous system engaged in the transmission and sharing of messages; and it demonstrates the validity of the library as a part both of the afferent and efferent nerve systems the afferent systems bringing information into the control centre and the efferent systems sending information outwards in the form of instructions and commands. But this reaching out to the nervous systems of others logically leads us to discuss another inexplicable the act of 'symbolization'—that is, an ability possessed by the human species to process sensory input in terms of symbols. This ability must be placed first in the history of the human ascent, even ahead of the fire and the axe. It is this ability which sometimes urges man to communicate across generations; to write books or construct monuments. This urge Aristotle called *Athanatidzein* or man's striving to break his confinement in time.

2.2 SYMBOLISM AND COMMUNICATION

One of the most tantalising areas of research relating to the human brain and the human cognitive processes is the way in which the brain seems to have this ability to process sensory input in terms of symbols: that is, of representing an entity not immediately present to the senses. This capability is peculiar to the human brain. Thinking implies symbols and the symbols themselves entail a 'pre-sharing', or a community of meaning however small, before these symbols can be used to bring one mind into contact with another. Once these symbols are used they can be stored and others initiated into their use: this heritage we call culture. But, in fact, the animal kingdom and the lower life forms do communicate in the sense of using signs to co-ordinate co-operative endeavour. We speak of ant 'societies', but whether we can say they have culture in the sense of a reservoir of symbols, with rules for their usage, is a very different matter. Konrad Lorenz (12) clearly differentiates between the kind of sign evident in the animal kingdom and that which man displays in his communicative activity:

No means of communication, no learning is ever handed down by tradition in animals. In other words animals have no culture.

The symbolic replication of experience would seem to be a faculty that is unique to man; though it is sometimes conceded that some animals, particularly dolphins, may have this in a limited form. What is unique, however, is the phenomenon which the neurologist calls 'cross modal association' (12); that is, the transference of information received by one sense modality to that of another. For example, a dog can be trained to react to a verbal symbol or word through the auditory mode, or his hearing. A word announcing

44

dinner or the return of his master will evoke a response, but he is incapable of transferring this symbolisation to his visual system. He cannot recognise a picture of a dinner or his master, let alone the printed word, though he will react to the auditory symbol or, of course, the physical presence of either.

This facility of transferring information from one sense mode to that of another is unique to man. Indeed, the expression of terms peculiar to one sense in that of another is a familiar poetic device known as 'synesthesia'. One of the best examples of synesthesia occurs in Baudelaire's sonnet *Correspondences* when he describes certain perfumes as 'soft as oboes, green as meadows'. Cross-modal association in man is often thought to be verbally mediated. When we appreciate a work of art or a piece of music, we must use words; this is, however, a very contentious area. In the human being, comprehension of the auditory symbol precedes its recognition as a written form; which is why storytelling, reading aloud and the vocabulary of the parents are so important in the child's linguistic and reading development (14).

This brings us to the point where 'signs' and 'symbols' have to be differentiated in some degree. In general terms, the sign is taken as a signal of the immediate presence of the referent. For instance, smoke is a sign of fire, or a blush may be a sign of embarrasment; though we may react to these signs in much the same way as we would react to the appropriate verbal symbols. If we accept the generic term 'signals' as comprising the whole range of signs and symbols by means of which the organism interacts with the environment, then animals live largely in a world of signs but man also interacts in a universe of symbols. In Susanne Langer's terms: the symbol is a substitute for the sign and can be used without the immediate presence of the referent. As von Frisch (15) has shown, the animal creation can have elaborate sign systems. The bee's dance, for example, indicates the proximity of honey, but the bee cannot indicate that there was honey there yesterday or that there will be honey tomorrow: the signal is bound within the realms of *immediacy*. The classic distinction is put by Langer (16):

To a clever dog the name of a person is a signal that the person is present; you say the name and he pricks up his ears and looks for the object. If you say 'dinner' he becomes restive expecting food. You cannot make any communication with him that is not taken as a signal of something immediately forthcoming, his brain is a direct transmitter of information from the world to his senses.

The human brain is more than a transmitter; it would seem to be more akin to a telephone exchange retaining and storing messages against the time they might be needed. Because symbols are the language of the human brain, man is able to form concepts and communicate them to others. These significant symbols are arbitrary and derive their communicative significance from shared conventions, so they enable man to create a reality far more subtle and complex than would be possible were he limited to the information contained in natural signs, like Susanne Langer's dog. Although he shares in the physical world of natural *signs*, he lives in the greater part of his mental life in a universe of symbols. Man has words for 'justice' 'love' 'honour'—all of which have no tangible referents in physical reality, yet support the imposing edifices of political theory, ethics and theology.

Again, Langer's dog lives directly in the 'here and now'; he does not know that there were dogs before him and that there will be dogs after him. Man, because of his faculty of symbolization, has a concept of events in sequence; he has a concept of time. From man's activity in a symbolic universe of his own creation comes the concept of the library; from his urge to transcend time comes the actuality of the library. This important cluster of concepts in the social foundations of librarianship can be represented as:

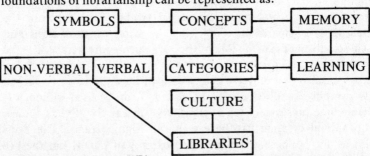

It would seem from the copious writings on this topic that man's superiority in the contest for self preservation is the result not only of his wider range of signals and his quicker learning power, but also of his ability to use signs to *indicate* things and to *represent* them. The use of these substitute signs is the essence of symbolism and our powers of reasoning; they can take the place of past experiences and feed the imagination by combining memories of things that might be in future experience, such an ability takes a man from the here and now. The development of language is the history of this gradual accumulation and elaboration of a special kind of symbol, the *word*; the development of libraries is a corollary to this social ability to store experiences for future use or futher creative imaginings.

No animal community can exist without a steering mechanism to guide the social relations of its members; this fascinating study lies at the intersection where zoology and psychology have combined to form the study of ethology, or animal behaviour, culminating in the more specialized field called by Sebeok (17) 'zoosemiotics': the study of sign behaviour in the animal kingdom.

Man's capacity for symbolic behaviour does, however, raise important questions both for theories of knowledge and theories of reality. Is there a difference between 'symbolic' reality and a 'real' reality which is 'out there'? What is the difference between mediated and direct experience? Traditional western philosophy held that reality was 'out there' like a great and infinite cosmic blackboard; and for a long time this concept misled classificationists like H E Bliss, who sought to compile a classification scheme which would reflect this order of knowledge. Knowledge was a given entity and man a passive receiver. The new approach to man which gives human perception the value of creative act is reflected in tacitly putting forward the thesis that reality is a social construction.

There is a strong school of thought in sociology which contends that reality is a symbolic construct: this school of thought is called the 'sociology of symbolic interaction'; a thesis which finds its most coherent expression in the work of Hugh Duncan (18). His major contention is that the communication of symbols is an essential part of the dynamic of society, and that the sociology of communication should concern itself with investigating the functions of symbolic communication in establishing social roles and the functions of society. One point of special notice here is the influence of dramatic theory on social thought. Some three and a half centuries after Shakespeare reflected that 'all the world's a stage and all the men and women merely players' (19), sociologists discovered that we are actors. We play roles, we react to symbolism—be it in the uniform of a traffic warden, the wig of a High Court judge, or to any other non-verbal indicator of a man's status in the social hierarchy. The symbols communicate to us because they modify or adjust our behaviour.

The other influence came from the famous philosopher of culture

47

Ernst Cassirer (20). His concept of man as the symbolizing animal led him to attempt a systematic synthesis of the whole range of human culture. No single one of the areas of language, myth, science, art or religion gives us direct and complete access to reality; rather they are different forms of apprehension which originate in primitive symbols and acts. Man does not find order and intelligibility in the world; his consciousness creates order and system. The categories of the understanding need no longer be deduced theoretically as Kant asserted, but are, in fact, social constructions. Therefore human experience is accounted for by the creativity of the human mind.

2.3 COMMUNICATION AND KNOWLEDGE

If we then accept the thesis that the vast construct of human knowledge is a complex edifice of symbols, it goes a long way towards explaining one of the main themes in contemporary western culture: the breakdown of communication between man and man as a by-product of the problem of knowledge. Different men use different symbolic systems to investigate their own particular aspects of reality and consequently find difficulties in communicating with each other. Here at last would seem to be a chance for a new kind of librarian with a new social role as 'linkman'; the man with the overview, whose particular expertise is a kind of 'knowledge about knowledge'; who realises the degree to which the major disciplines of knowledge fragment and overlap each other. This is an area to which educationalists are now beginning to devote some attention. After all, the concept of discipline was originally an educational device for organizing the transmission of the cultural legacy from one generation to the next, and it is a concept which has had a stultifying effect upon library classification schemes. The boundaries of disciplines change while the main class structure of the classification scheme remains rigid, with the consequence that every subject specialist sees his own cherished domain fragmented and distorted. Any college librarian will vouch for this communication problem.

In an attempt to form some kind of synthesis for the educationist, Philip Phenix (21) classified the disciplines of human knowledge according to six basic types of realms of meaning. Each of these areas is characterized by having a distinct logical form of symbolic structure together with a separate methodology of enquiry. This approach is a breakaway from the traditional subject matter curriculum, taking as a criterion the realm of meaning rather than the content. In this way he attempts to solve the problem of, say, the

48

superiority of science over poetry. The answer is: they cannot be *meaningfully* compared; they both use different rules in their approach to reality. When Wordsworth says: 'Ten thousand saw I at a glance', his intent is not to give a scientific enumeration of the daffodils, but to express a poetic truth; and, in indexing terms, the 'distributed relative' is a testimony to the fact that the daffodil can be viewed in different ways by painter, botanist and poet.

Each subject uses language in a different way, and within different realms of meaning. Language, then, is no mere inventory of the items of experience, instead, different ways of organizing experience and these differences have their bases in the distinctive histories, environmental settings, cultural and genetic histories of the speech communities among whom the particular languages develop. The meanings of the word used depend upon the crystallisation of the person's experience to whom it is used. The term 'dog' to an Eskimo may probably denote 'husky'; and the same term may denote a poodle to the middle class dowager of Park Lane; each interprets according to their cultural experience. Edward Sapir expresses the relativity of language in the famous Whorf-Sapir hypothesis:

The relation between thought and language is often misunderstood. Language is not merely a systematic inventory of the various items of experience which seem relevant to the individual as is so often supposed, but is a self-contained creative symbolic organization which not only refers to experience but actually defines experience for us....(22)

There is little doubt regarding the relationship between vocabulary and perception; languages differ notoriously in vocabulary and this difference is generally correlated with a difference in environment. Thus Whorf (23) notices that the Eskimo languages have a variety of words for different kinds of snow, where we have only one; here perception and survival are interdependent. Similarly the Paiute, a desert people, speak a language that permits the most detailed description of topographical features—a necessity in an environment where the location of water holes is of paramount importance. The Whorf-Sapir thesis, although lacking the status of universal acceptance, does point to the conclusion that language constitutes a sort of logic, or as it were a general frame of reference for the perceiving mind; moulding the thought of its users and so accounting for the communication problems between cultures.

49

Such ways of looking at the world are important, not only for environmental details, but also for logic and metaphysics. Classical logic took the subject-predicate form of statement as basic, and insisted that any logical manipulations be confined to this form; a policy not without influence in the retrieval techniques of the librarian. One of the most fascinating strands in the history of western thought is the ambivalent attitude manifested towards language. The assertion of St John that in the beginning was the word, has sometimes been taken in an over literal way, for it is to the *logos* that western civilization owes much of its verbal emphasis. Even to the average man today, it provides the root and bark of his experience and he cannot easily transcend the boundaries of his language. The other side of the coin is shown in the attempt to move away from bounds of language and to strain after the ineffable in the tranquillity of total silence. In this, the Trappist ideal (24) seems to have a parallel with the Zen *Koan*, 'you know the sound of two hands clapping, what is the sound of one?' In the construction and investigation of reality the word, like the book which gave it permanent fom, is the paramount medium for the creation, symbolization and communication of experience.

The classical and Christian philosophers used words to order and docket reality. Libraries held the recorded sum of human experience, exemplified in the great areas of human intellectual endeavour — literature, philosophy, theology, law and history — although the verbal mode was not the only form of communicative expression as can be seen from their interest in iconography and music. It is significant that, after the seventeenth century, there was a marked divergence from the use of language in the solution of problems, or as George Steiner (25) called it, 'a retreat from the word'. Up to that time the predominant bias and content of the natural sciences was descriptive, and mathematics was mainly linked to the empirical world. After the early developments by Newton and Leibnitz, mathematics became a fantastically rich and complex language, less and less tied to empirical reality, and constructing elaborate edifices of form and meaning: a new symbolic world from which the innumerate would be excluded. Between the mathematical symbol and the language of common usage the communication channels became increasingly blocked, and both languages became untranslateable one into the other. Mathematics was no longer a shorthand for verbal propositions: indeed, as

Bertrand Russell (26) tells us, many of the concepts and relations dealt with in the field of mathematics have no equivalents in tangible reality.

The communication implications of this fact are that man's experience and perceptions are split into two separate domains, and one of the distinctive features in the growth of any discipline is the gradual submission of its concepts and techniques to mathematical measurement. The social sciences are a prime example of this. Sociology started as a descriptive science and now glories in the making of mathematical models, in multivariate analysis and middle range theory. In the realm of the biological sciences, Sir Darcy Wentworth Thompson (27) could combine the gifts of poet and mathematician without any fears of schizoid contradiction; but now the science of genetics has become practically closed to the layman who does not have a grounding in statistical theory, as a cursory reading of Watson's (28) work will show. The word is giving way to number, and even in librarianship the urge to quantify has become dominant.

The great danger in the universe of knowledge is that the realms of meaning have become hermitically sealed specialisms, none of which attempts to communicate with each other or with the lay public. There would seem to be an urgent need for a popularising journalism, in the best sense of the term, which can bring home to the layman the social implications of these studies. The political dangers of an intellectual elite, immune from criticism of responsibility, does not need much emphasis. Between the two symbolic worlds of word and number there exists an ever widening gulf of incomprehension and, often, of hostility.

The early sixties (29) saw the ignoble controversy between C P Snow (30) and F R Leavis, which was a glaring symptom of the cultural squint which the growth of knowledge has forced on western man. The 'two cultures' controversy was sparked off by C P Snow in the 1959 Rede Lecture at Cambridge. Snow deplored the even-widening gap between the humanities and technology, and the wilful and even proud ignorance of the non-scientists in all things scientific. To Snow, no man can properly be claimed to be educated unless he can understand, for example, the second law of thermodynamics as well as being able to read and appreciate Shakespeare. This gap between the 'two cultures' is, according to Snow, an unmitigated disaster for a technological society.

But these two approaches to reality are complementary, not antithetical. They correspond to the two types of mentality put forward by Liam Hudson (31), as 'divergent' and 'convergent' thinkers. However, the notion of essential literacy is still rooted in the values of verbal discourse, and men who say things tend to be in charge of men who do things. Biologists and psychologists have not been idle in trying to find a neurological basis for the explanation of these two modes of thinking. Of particular interest in this field is the work of Robert Ornstein (32). Central to his thesis is the hypothesis of the bifunctional brain in man. The left hemisphere of the brain (connected to the right side of the body) is predominantly involved with analytical and logical thinking. This hemisphere seems to process information sequentially and it controls the verbal and mathematical skills usually measured by IQ tests. The right hemisphere is responsible for orientation in space, artistic creativity and self awareness and, compared with the sequential and analytical operations of the left side, that of the right seems to be more intuitive and more instantaneous. He does emphasize the complementarity in these two modes of thinking which makes this gap in communication even more poignant.

One gets the feeling that there is the danger of a false dilemma here: portraying the artists as intuitive and the scientist as coldly logical; in some sense one feels that this is a bogus debate. What is even more worrying is the communication gap between those who are restricted in their daily communication to the same verbal mode: I refer here to the problems of communication between social classes. Not every human being has the same area of experience or the same share in the riches of his culture. This melancholy fact has haunted the egalitarian educationist and social radical for some time.

Since the war, in most western countries a major slogan of educational planners has been equality in education as a major factor in forming a more egalitarian society. Raymond Boudon (33) gives a pessimistic account of these efforts and points out that, whereas all western societies have been characterised by a steady increase in educational opportunity since 1945, inequality of special opportunity has remained almost completely stable. The probability of a manual worker's son achieving a higher social status is still as low as it was. What is more, Boudon constructs a model based on the major research findings in educational and social opportunity, and uses this model to predict that, even if cultural inequalities were totally eliminated, there would still be a substantial disparity between working and middle class children in terms of their chances to benefit from the educational system. His model generates the conclusion that the key to social inequality lies not in educational but in economic inequality.

It can be argued that the problems of economic inequality are not a primary concern of the librarian, but he is involved in the problems of 'compensatory education' which intends to widen the opportunities of the culturally deprived. There is evidence of this commitment in the many 'outreach activities' engaged in by innovative librarians and as a prominent British practitioner, Janet Hill, puts it: 'For the librarian who is community-minded there are no limits to the possibilities of working through the community both inside and outside the confines of library buildings.' This is a philosophy of librarianship which entails bringing books to children wherever they be—in park playground, sports centre or housing estate. It consists of bringing to the deprived the benefits of a puppet show, or the intellectual stimulus of listening to a story which has an important effect on the linguistic and future reading ability of the child. As we have seen from the earlier sections in this chapter, language ability is vital.

The investigations of Basil Bernstein have shown that the manual labouring classes in Britain use a different and more restricted language than that of the middle classes. The working class child grows up in an atmosphere of linguistic impoverishment, the vocabulary of the parents is restricted and so he labours under a disadvantage in a social system which places a high value on verbal facility. This type of code Bernstein (35) calls a 'restricted code'; it is mainly context-tied and lacks a generalised meaning or an ability to manipulate abstractions. The middle class child has access to an 'elaborate code', to a wider universe of meaning, and is consequently enabled to adapt to changes in knowledge and thought with greater ease. The communication relevance of these codes can be seen in the editorial of the popular tabloid newspaper, which restricts its vocabulary to personalised vocabulary-controlled accounts of mainly human issues, compared with an editorial in the *Times, Telegraph* or *Guardian*. Knowledge, communication and culture are indeed three interlocking concepts and Bernstein puts the communication problem cogently:

The class structure influences educational roles and brings families into a special relationship with each other and deeply penetrates the structure of life experiences within the family. The class system has deeply marked the distribution of knowledge within society. It has given different access to the world that is permeable; it has sealed off communities from each other and has ranked these communities on a scale of invidious worth (36).

The growing lack of communication between social groups is of direct relevance to the public librarian, and an awareness of this would seem to provide an operational blueprint for an excursion by him into the problems of social communication and an understanding of the missing three quarters of the population—those who do not use public library services. In 1958, Dr Joseph Trenaman (37) undertook a large-scale enquiry into the attitudes of the adult population towards educational opportunities and sources of information. He found that no more than ten per cent could be credited with any sustained interest in the cultural opportunities provided by books, periodicals, newspapers and broadcasting. The great majority of this group had an education of an advanced and academic type.

A further twenty per cent of the group investigated had only a little secondary or part time education and in this group one could assume only a comparatively simple background of knowledge and a limited vocabulary. Nevertheless this group was prepared to take note of serious matter presented in a simple and straightforward way. But the third element, amounting to some twenty five per cent and consisting mainly of semi-skilled workers, were interested in those things which had relevance to their immediate affairs, providing this information could be presented to them in concrete terms and through people—this justifying the journalistic maxim of Arthur Christiansen (38) of the *Daily express*: 'always tell stories through people and never deal with abstractions'. Below this group lay a fundamental dividing line, 'the point where indifference changes to a mild curiosity to know more of the world about one'.

Nearly forty five per cent of the sample fell below this threshold, forming an amorphous mass 'resistant to new ideas and higher values'. One of the most difficult and potentially explosive situations is that caused by communication barriers between one social class and another, and any sociology of librarianship will need to investigate with some degree of rigour how the library as a social agency can function as a channel in this difficult area of social communication.

2.4 COMMUNICATION AND CULTURE

The essence of man's nature is the capacity to share in the transmitted legacy of social experience which is expressed in symbolic form; and a further extension of this capacity is his ability to influence and change this legacy by the contributions of his own perception: ;. Through the media of communication, the private experiences of the individual are made public, and contribute to the common world picture. This assertion, and its implications for the social role of the library, will necessarily involve us in a discussion of the concepts of culture and social change. Some difficulties may arise at the outset of such a discussion: there is the literary concept of culture put forward by Matthew Arnold (39) which is the one most frequently found in common usage:

Culture being a pursuit of our total perfection by means of getting to know, on all matters which most concern us, the best which has been thought and said in the world.

This, is an evaluative definition which is usually implied when we speak of a person as 'cultured', and is often a source of confusion to the student. The standard definition is the one put forward by E B Tylor (40): 'That complex whole which includes knowledge, art, belief, morals or any other capabilities acquired by man as member of society'. What must be emphasized is that culture is a human construction, necessarily synthetic because it is not biologically given, and continually undergoing change. In its broadest sense it refers to the total repertoire of human action and its products, and in Berger's (41) terms it forms the distinction between that which is *genetically* transmitted, and that which is *socially* transmitted through the learning process.

But what of this sociological abstraction which we call 'society', and what is its relevance for communication? The answer is that both are part of the definiton of man; a fundamental attribute expressed by Aristotle (42) when he said that the man who can live without society 'must be either a beast or a god'; that is, the person who is incapable of sharing a common life is either above or below humanity. Man is dependent upon others for his ability to communicate, for warmth and for shelter; unlike the animal, his growth and maturation extends over a lengthy period, and in the achieving of this maturation he is dependent upon other minds and upon a changing network of communication. As McIver (43) expresses it:

'Society is a system of usages and procedures, of authority and mutual aid, of many groupings and divisions of controls of human behaviour and of liberties. It is the web of social relationships and it is always changing.'

Society cannot exist without communication, and communication assumes a social network. Neither process can be treated meaningfully by itself. In fact, for the anthropologist, Edward Hall (44), 'culture is communication, communication is culture', wo when we speak of the library as a cultural agency we automatically analyse it as an instrument of communication.

2.5 THE SELF AND COMMUNICATION

The life history of man as communicator starts with his assimilation of the norms and standards of his cultural setting. From the moment of his birth he imbibes with his mother's milk the ways of knowing, doing, and believing peculiar to his social group. The most important factor in his environment is other people. To be sure he will need favourable physical surroundings to sustain himself and provide for his comfort and physical well being; but the importance of other people lies in the fact that they provide social models upon which to frame his own concent of 'self'. This is an interactive process in the sense that the individual builds others which in turn helps to fashion him as a social being. When he enters a library he comes into contact with the ideas and life styles of significant contemporaries and famous ancestors.

To regard the individual and society as antithetical, or to regard society as Rousseau did, as something superimposed upon the person is a grave mistake. The individuals who develop without the social contact of others do so in grotesque ways; the antropologists call them 'feral children' and there is an extensive literature on this phenomenon. In almost all cases of 'wild' or 'feral' children, the concept of selfhood was completely absent and they had to be trained to speak, eat and dress. The point which emerges here is that the individual and his *humanity* are entirely dependent upon society, and without society there is no individual.

Perhaps the most poignant account of an individual cut off from communication with society is the case of Helen Keller (44) who, deprived of sight and hearing in early infancy, describes in her autobiography an existence in which the main communication

56

channels were blocked. The manual alphabet invented by her nurse was her only contact with social reality and she describes her frustration and rage when her personal need to communicate was thwarted; a similar trait is manifested in autistic children. The essential point is, however, that we need a concept of *self*, before we can communicate with others. The necessity of this interaction can be illustrated further if we look at the way in which a young child acquires the communication symbols used in his group.

As Sullivan (45) points out, as soon as an infant picks up a verbal trick such as saying 'mama', he receives a response from the adult. From this response he gets the idea of the power implicit in this accomplishment. He learns the meaning of the symbols from the responses others make and in this way he builds up his communication repertoire, giving a social value to the creative or play element in his nature. When we think, we communicate with our 'self' and indeed we often rehearse the message before its transmission. The child uses symbols which have an area of meaning for himself and he assumes they will arouse a similar response in others. George Mead, whose work provides the *locus classicus* for this argument puts it thus (47):

It is of course the relationship of this symbol this vocal gesture to such a set of responses in the individual himself as well as in the other that makes of that vocal gesture what I call a "significant symbol". A symbol does tend to call out in the other a group of reactions such as it tends to call out in the communicator. This is what, of course, is involved in what we term the meaning of a thing or its significance.

According to Mead's reasoning the 'significant symbol' pre-supposes some form of *sharing* and also an expectation that the same response will be invoked in the source as in the receiver. One doubts if this ever happens with any rigorous degree of exactitude and will differ according to the aspect of reality under discussion. The term calorimeter may evoke the same image among two scientists irrespective of their cultural backgrounds; the concept of 'poverty' may encounter communication difficulties in its 'transfer', from the head of one social scientist to the head of another. The greater the area of shared public knowledge, or as Ziman (48) would call it, 'consensus', the greater the ease of communication; and this resultant stability of terminology has an acute relevance in the bibliographical control of recorded knowledge.

Nevertheless, information is transmitted by an individual to himself and he uses a kind of 'mirror image' to test a message before transmission; a phenomenon known as 'covert rehearsal' (49). It is of the utmost importance in understanding the communication process to note that the individual is a self-communicating system as well as a component in communication networks with others. This may well be the way to approach the problem of individual creativity or 'inventive information' as when the self-reflecting individual encodes one level of experience into another, or in letting the mind wander freely over a problem, brings together two completely disparate frames of reference—a process which Koestler (50) calls 'bisociation', and one which he considers to be the basis of creativity.

Because communication is the means by which one person influences another and, is in turn, influenced by him, it is the actual carrier of the social process. In this sense we distinguish between 'communication' as a *primary* process, that is language, gesture and commicative behaviour, and 'communications', with the final's'. The latter term denotes the secondary processes such as the print and electronic media and, by implication, libraries. Communications serve the function of maintaining surveillance on society and its environment, and of disclosing threats and opportunities which might affect the members of that society. Just as the primitive tribes had watchers on the hillsides to act as a warning system, so the modern electronic media conduct searching enquiries into current problems through the medium of news broadcasts and documentaries; the same is true of the newspaper. In the same way the special library acts as an early warning system for its clientele, alerting them to changes in the subject environment.

The social inheritance must be transmitted if man is to survive. Without this transmission we are not social beings, as we have noted in the case of feral children. If such a heritage were to be destroyed then we would relapse into barbarism. The knowledge system of society depends upon this transmission of concepts and skills from one generation to the next. The functions of the communications system are, in Lasswell's (51) terse phrase, that of 'watcher, forum and teacher'. In cybernetic terms, society's networks of communication channels help to reduce entropy and to keep the social system from running down, and the library as a storage system is an important part of this entropy reducing network. The important corollary here, is that such storage systems are *static* and useless if they remain unused; but once they come into contact with the enquiring mind they become kinetic in the form of potential knowledge.

The book as a communications medium is merely a source of these stimuli or sense data; it becomes an information source when it is integrated into the concept system of the individual, and acts as a guide to future behaviour, or in some way re-structures the perceptions of the person who is *informed*. The selection and reception of the information will depend upon the individual's conception of his own needs; one man's information is another man's noise; or what another man knows already may be a source of information to me and completely restructures my perception of the world.

For the general social channels whereby information is diffused through society, Pierce Butler (52) postulates the following:

1 *Education*: including adult education, where the transmission system of the primitive tribe has become formalized in the education system as we know it.

2 What he calls the *'consultation process'* or the function by which the learned professions, such as law, medicine and engineering, organize a particular problem area of social reality and act as mediators in helping other members of that society. In this they play the role of professional expert *vis a vis* the client.

3 Mass communications make it possible for every citizen to be *continuously* exposed to a torrent of information concerning current happenings and events; they may often try to take over the function of the professional in recommending solutions to problems or in attempting to modify individual behaviour.

4 *The interpersonal communication process*. Perhaps the most powerful agency of all comprising gossip, rumour and information passed from mouth to mouth.

5 Butler also adds the category of *reference work* as a possible channel. I would tend to subsume this under the interpersonal process as I shall hope to demonstrate in the next chapter. What is interesting is to attempt to analyse the role of *libraries* in the general sense of a social agency and *librarianship* in the sense of an active profession giving a service and *mediating* between the client and the library as information store.

That the library is for society what the memory is for the individual is an analogy which is often used, but the psychological corollary to this analogy is seldom underlined: that the human memory is not a passive instrument, as Frances Yates (53) has shown in her classic work on the subject. It selects, sifts and editorialises the experiences of the individual and thus serves as the foundation of creative thought. This is an important point when drawing an analogy between the library as social memory and the memory of the individual; there is danger of being misleading if one implies that the memory is simply an inert repository or some kind of psychic dustbin. Concepts are not stored in the human memory like peas in a bag, but co-ordinated, classified and constantly changing in the light of a new sensory input. This is the point where the importance of classification as a communicative device can be impressed upon the student, providing a foundation for later studies. Like the human memory, the incoming materials are related to the store of concepts already in the library store, not coded according to a classification scheme in the abstract sense of the term.

Communication is not something remote from our daily lives, nor from the purpose and practice of librarianship. Communication is something we do by virtue of the fact that we are social beings, and librarianship is a natural and logical extension of this activity. It follows, then, that every librarian should have some elementary training in sociological analysis as part of his education. In essence, society is a network of shared understanding so that evey discipline concerned with society must also deal with communication; and, as we reason from the premise that librarianship is a social discipline, we must needs be concerned with communication in all its aspects. The only danger here is in giving the impression that society is a static entity or, in some vague way, just a multiplicity of social groups and institutions; whereas it is an ongoing dynamic process which is being re-created at each moment because of the interaction between human beings.

An example of this fallacious belief can be found in the frontispiece of a work by the seventeenth century philosopher Thomas Hobbes—*The Leviathan*—in which he puts forward an account of the origin of human society. On this prontispiece is a gigantic figure composed of multitudes of life-sized figures conceived of as atoms in a larger whole. Although this may typify a crowd, it does not describe society. Every single act of social behaviour necessarily involves communication, *ie* the interaction of one mind with that of another. This communication, in order to be effective, entails a *shared* understanding of what a word, look, action or gesture will mean; in other words we must share *common symbols*. The next point to emphasise is that communication is not an amenity nor an optional extra; we communicate whether we wish to or not. It is an essence which makes the person what he is. The need to communicate is just as much a part of man as his biological needs; if you starve a baby he will die, similarly, if you cut him off from all communicative contact he will progress little beyond the stage of the animal.

Communication then is the carrier of the social process; it organizes, stabilizes and modifies our social life and it enables us to pass on its forms and meanings from one generation to the next. That which we call the social process—our daily activities of knowing, acting, believing and interacting with each other— depends upon the accumulation, transmission and diffusion of knowledge. But knowledge in turn depends upon communication, and in this way the library acts as a medium in the transmission process. Every baby is born into an ongoing system of skills, beliefs, ideas and values: and this repository we call *culture*.

2.7 HOW DO CULTURE AND KNOWLEDGE INTERACT?

Although there are very many definitions of culture it is usually more helpful to say what it *does*, rather than what it *is*. It serves as a medium through which human minds interact with each other in communication. This idea of culture may be compared with the idea of light in physics. Banesh Hoffman, the physicist, in a very readable and interesting book (53), tells how the Greeks realised that there must be something bridging the distance between our eyes and the things we see, so they gave it an objective reality and set about studying it and inventing theories about it. Although the poet John Donne tells us that 'no man is an island', in fact he is until communication through the medium of culture bridges the gap between his mind and that of another.

Culture provides a field of reference so that the individual can organise his world: the culture into which we are born greatly influences our perceptions, consequently people from different cultures will often see things that outsiders might miss. For instance, the Eskimo depends upon his knowledge of snow for his survival, and, therefore, he will see the different gradations of snow that a city man might miss completely. Culture also provides the rules for communication and human interaction. Being a part of a culture

61

means that one knows the rules of that culture. If one plays tennis or squash with someone, one relies on his accepting and knowing the rules of the game; one may even be able to anticipate his tactics, since there is the sharing of common culture.

It is noteworthy how there is always a feeling of uncertainty when we encounter someone from a strange culture; the *symbols* and *rules* of communication are unfamiliar, and in terms of information theory uncertainty is at its greatest. We cannot predict his reactions to certain situations and this uncertainty influences our own behaviour making it stiff and formal and, as far as he is concerned, we may even seem aggressive. Inter-cultural communication problems are very much the concern of the librarian, particularly with reference to comparative librarianship.

The concept of 'self' is of the utmost importance in communication and it is because we can reflect on ourselves that we can more readily identify with the experience of others, even more so if they share our own particular culture. This factor often displays a negative side, as when people react more readily to violence in a neighbouring city or state, because they share the same culture as the people there, and evince a complete indifference to the warfare in a distant land. Culture and society develops our concept of self-hood through the social means provided by the agency of the family, the school and what the sociologist would call 'reference groups'. Society also helps us to recognise that, although the subjective experiences of another person will never be identical to our own, they will be recognisably similar. This faculty is sometimes called 'the moral imagination' or 'empathic communication' and is the basis for the ethical maxim of 'Do unto others as you would have them do unto you'—not forgetting the cynical warning of Geroge Bernard Shaw that their 'tastes may not be similar'.

We have seen that the individual is a biological organism and that, on a higher level, society can also be treated as an organic model. Human society has long been a self-regulating system, preserving itself by conveying information to its members and obtaining information from them. Man, as we have discussed earlier, is an information processing system, and to survive he communicates with his environment. He receives information through his senses and each of these senses gives him a different quality of information, though normally they work together to give him a multi-dimensional picture of the world.

62

There is a helpful analogy in treating the library as an organism and comparing it with the human intellectual processes. The library receives incoming sense data in the form of materials, and they are classified and encoded according to the rules of an already existent memory store. So also man organises the data of experience into categories and classes of things. Man perceives according to his needs. That is, he selects from available stimuli and rejects others; so also the library as an organism selects materials according to its terms of reference and rejects other items from the multiplicity of materials available. Like the individual the library is, or should be, an open system in continual interaction with its environment.

To delineate the relationship between the library and human knowledge let us take, for example, a hypothetical primitive tribe; the kind of society which the anthropologist and historian would call pre-literate. The skills of the tribe relating to hunting, fishing, building huts and other survival activities will be passed from father to son. The ritual and magical techniques for placating the gods and gaining their favour in attaining spiritual control over their environment would probably be in the hands of the 'wiseman' of the tribe who would be a kind of social memory, or primaeval counterpart of the reference librarian. All this knowledge would be passed on in a rather haphazard way which later modern societies would formalize into professions such as education, engineering, law, medicine and so on. The sum total of their culture might be summarized as follows:

Knowing how: The skills of hunting, fishing, skinning animals, building huts, all the ways of coping with their environment. We might call this primitive technology or material culture, rather analogous to the sciences and applied sciences in the Dewey Decimal Classification scheme.

Believing or *Knowing why*: The tribe's ideas about life after death, their value systems, taboos or rules of behaviour; we can call this their *non-material culture*. The knowledge possessed by each member of the tribe would be drawn from this pool of ideas about ways of doing, acting and believing. In order to survive, this culture must be transmitted from one generation to the next and diffused among the members of the tribe; so culture, knowledge and communication are interdependent entities held together through the medium of *symbols*.

Why then libraries and librarianship? We have mentioned the old 'wiseman' of the tribe, as the anthropologist would call him. He functions as a memory bank for all the important things, but he would later be supplanted when men came to record their knowledge in symbolic form. In order to provide channels for the spread of information, society creates special instruments which it calls *institutions*. Examples of social institutions are the family, the church, the professions and latterly, the mass media. They are the blocks out of which the edifice of society is built. The library as an information store is not an institution as such, but rather an *agency* or *channel*. Agencies in society usually function as instruments for the expression of the aims of an institution acting as a physical embodiment of an idea, for instance, we think of law as an institution and the court as an agency; or religion as an institution and the churches as agencies. We can see the library in terms of Lasswell's communication model thus:

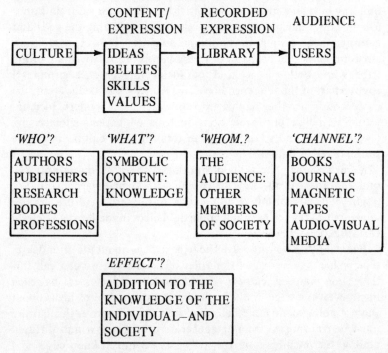

As we can see, the function of the library changes, but in each case it is a channel or agency acting as a storage unit and means of diffusion. It can also act as a *source* with the librarian as mediator:

LIBRARY	LIBRARIAN	ENQUIRER
as	as	as
INFORMATION STORE	MEDIATOR	CLIENT

If the librarian is to become an effective mediator between man and the graphic records, or as the sociologist calls them the 'social transcript', he must possess much more than the vocational skills necessary for the organization of knowledge; he must also have a certain knowledge about the various disciplines and the role of knowledge in society. Jesse Shera (54) calls this study 'social epistemology' meaning the effect of knowledge on society: a kind of opposite of the study called the sociology of knowledge, which is the study of the effect of social conditions upon the knowledge systems of society. They are both important parts of a librarian's education, since knowledge does not exist in an abstract sense as 'something out there', there must be a *knower*; it is an entity that has to evolve in response to human needs. It is a creation of the human mind which again re-creates the sum of human experience; that is, most people in some small way leave the world a little better than they found it.

1 George Miller 'The human links in communication systems' *Proceedings of the National Electronics Conference* 12, 1959, p 395-40

2 J Z Young *Doubt and certainty in science; a biologists reflections on the brain* Oxford, Clarendon Press, 1950. This model is further developed in his *Model of the brain* London, Oxford University Press, 1967.

3 John Locke *Essay concerning the nature of human understanding* 1690.

4 Karl Popper *Objective knowledge* London, Oxford University Press, 1972.

5 William Wordsworth *Intimations of immortality*.

6 A E Housman *More poems* XII

7 Sir Russell Brain *The nature of experience* London, Oxford University Press, 1959, p 46.

8 J Z Young *Doubt and certainty in science* Oxford, Clarendon Press, 1950.

9 *Op cit* p 61. There is a lucid and controversial discussion of this problem by the physiologist Richard Gregory in the *Times literary supplement* 3,764, 23 April 1974, p 429-30.

10 Michael Polanyi *Personal knowledge* London, Routledge and Kegan Paul, 1962 also his introductory work *The study of man* Chicago University Press, 1958.

11 Karl Popper *Objective knowledge* p 74ff.

12 Konrad Lorenz *On aggression* New York, Harcourt, Brace and World, 1966, p 40.

13 Mary A Brazier 'Neurophysiological contributions to the human communication' *in* F X Dance *Human communication theory* New York, Holt, Rinehart and Winston, 1968.

14 M M Lewis *Language and the child* London, National Foundation for Educational Research, 1969.

15 Karl von Frisch *The bees: their vision, chemical sense and language* New York, Cornell University Press, 1956.

16 Susanne Langer *Philosophy in a new key: study in the symbolism of reason, rite and art* Cambridge (Mass) Harvard University Press, 1967, p 30.

17 Thomas A Sebeok Aspects of anumal communication: the bees and the porpoises' *ETC: a review of general semantics* 24 (1) March 1967, p 59-83.

18 Hugh Duncan *Communication and social order* New York, Bedminster Press, 1966

19 William Shakespeare *As you like it* Act 2, scene 7.

20 Ernst Cassiere *Philosophy of symbolic forms* Yale University Press, 1959-69, 5 vols.

21 Philip Penix *Realms of meaning* New York, McGraw Hill, 1966.

22 Edward Sapir 'Conceptual categories of primitive languages' *Science* 74, 1931, p 578.

23 Benjamin Lee Whorf *Language thought and reality* edited by J B Carroll, Cambridge (Mass), MIT Press, 1956.

24 Thomas Merton *Elected silence* London, Burns and Oates, 1954.

25 George Steiner 'The retreat from the word' in *Language and Silence* London, Faber, 1958.

26 Bertrand Russell *Human knowledge: its scope and limits* London, Allen and Unwin, 1948.

27 Sir Darcy Wentworth Thompson *On growth and form* Cambridge, Cambridge University Press, 1942.

28 J D Watson *The double helix* London, Weidenfeld and Nicholson, 1958.

29 M Yudkin *and* F R Leavis *The two cultures debate* London, Chatto and Windus, 1962.

30 C P Snow *The two cultures: a second look* London, Oxford University Press, 1964.

31 Liam Hudson *Contrary imaginations* Harmondsworth, Penguin Books, 1966.

32 Robert Ornstein *The psychology of consciousness* New York, Freeman, 1972.

33 Raymond Boudon *Education opportunity and social inequality* New York , Wiley, 1974.

34 Janet Hill *Children are people: librarians in the community* London, Hamish Hamilton, 1973, p 63.

35 Basil Bernstein *Class, codes and control* London, Routledge and Kegan Paul, 1971.

36 *idem* 'Language and socialisation' *in* Noel Minnis ed *Linguistics at large* London, Gollancz, 1972, p 231.

37 Joseph Trenaman *Communication and comprehension:* report of an investigation by statistical methods of the effective communication of educative material and an assessment of the factors making for such communication. Longmans, 1967.

38 Arthur Christiansen *Headlines all my life* London, Heinemann, 1961.

39 Matthew Arnold *Culture and anarchy* London, Faber, 1966

40 E B Tyler *The origins of culture* New York, Harper, 1966.

41 P Berger *and* T Luckmann *The social construction of reality* London, Allen Lane, 1967.

42 Aristotle *The politics* book 1.

43 R M McIver *Society: an introductory analysis* London, MacMillan, 1965 p 5.

44 Edward T Hall *Silent language* New York, Doubleday, 1966.

45 Helen Keller *The story of my life* 1902.

46 Harry S Sullivan *Concepts of modern psychiatry* Washington, Anson Foundation, 1947.

47 George Mead *Mind, self and society from the standpoint of a social behaviourist* Chicago University Press, 1934 p 89.

48 J Ziman *Public knowledge: the social dimensions of science* London, Cambridge University Press, 1969.

49 George Mead *op cit.*

50 Arthur Koestler *The act of creation* London, Heinemann, 1964.

51 Harold Lasswell 'The structure and function of communication' *in* Leon Bryson *The communication of ideas* 1948.

52 Pierce Butler *Scholarship and civilization* Chicago, Chicago University Post-Graduate Librarianship School, 1944.

53 Banesh Hoffman *The strange story of the quantum* Harmondsworth, Penquin Books, 1963.

54 Jesse Shera *Sociological foundations of librarianship* London, Asia Publishing House, 1971, p 85.

CHAPTER 3

The inter-personal
communication process

IN THE first two chapters I have put forward areas of study which attempt to provide an answer to the following questions:

What are the ways in which individuals and societies acquire knowledge; and what are the ways by which knowledge is disseminated? How does the knowledge which an individual assimilates become part of a collective heritage of a culture? What purpose does the library serve in the network of social communication?

3.1 CONCEPT FORMATION AND COMMUNICATION

In terms of the communication models in chapter one, this chapter attempts to analyse the complex interactions of the *source* and the *receiver*: basic questions which confront the librarian in his professional practice.

We ask ourselves what is the nature of that psycho-physical process which takes place when a human mind confronts a library store and the bibliographic tools that provide a key to it? And finally, what happens when the enquirer encounters the librarian acting as *mediator* between the individual and those graphic records that provide the social transcript of his culture? We attempt to pursue Shera's paraphrase of Pope's famous couplet that, 'the proper study of librarianship is man' (1).

According to Berlo (2), there are five communication skills. Two of these are encoding skills, speaking and writing; two of them are decoding skills, reading and listening. The fifth is crucial to both encoding and decoding, and that is thought or reasoning. Philosophers and psychologists have long debated the question: what is the thinking process? Plato (3), always imaginative and ingenious, introduced the notion that thought required mental symbols and that these were 'images' that a man carried round with him. He argued that when we wanted to think about the physical world, our thought units became small visual replicas of the object they represented, received and kept intact by the retina of the eye.

This theory, although rather naive, was not radically altered until the beginning of this century when psychologists like Wertheimer (4) took up the position that thought did not require images at all; it required the manipulation of symbols, and these symbols must be related to our own experience. George Berkeley, the eighteenth century Irish philosopher was groping after this idea when he stoutly asserted that our experience is tied to concrete objects: when we think of 'man' we are forced to think of 'white or black, or a tawny or straight, or a crooked man, a tall or low or middle sized man' (5). It is difficult, if not impossible, to think without using concepts tied to our own experience.

This incursion into the processes of thinking inevitably brings us to a discussion on the nature of conceptual thought and language. Such questions as: what are the major sets of symbols that are available to us? And; what are our units of thought? One school of thought, particularly Gaston Viaud (6), asserts that reasoning in man is due to conceptual thought whose basic elements are concepts. A concept is a generalized and abstract symbol; in fact it is the sum of our knowledge of a particular class of objects. Being abstract it contains, or rather allows us to recall, the characteristic properties of the class of objects it represents and all the attributes which distinguish that class from others. For example, the concept 'dog' is the sum total of the properties that distinguish the dog from other animals: it is mammal, it hunts, barks, guards sheep and so on. The communiction source, Mr A, when starting a discourse with the receiver Mr B, will be influenced by the concept of dog derived from his own experience. If Mr A lives in Park Lane and Mr B is a denizen of the frozen wastes of the Polar North then the symbol 'dog' will mean different things to both. Thus my concept 'dog' includes all I know about dogs; my concept 'house', all I know about houses. In short, a concept is a condensation of experience in the act of interpersonal communication.

The psycholinguistic school represented by Whorf (7), would suggest that the major units of thought are *units of language*; this thesis is supported by the fact that we have difficulty in thinking about things for which we have no names. The question then arises: can we have wordless thoughts? The writings of Michael Polanyi (8)

69

and his theory of 'inarticulate knowledge' put forward the idea that we know more than we can say. In essence, the Whorfian hypothesis states that a person's language will not only determine what he thinks, but also what he perceives and the methods that he uses to communicate and arrive at decisions. The hypothesis, though it is not without critics, has a solid empirical backing. If we have no word for the white stuff that falls on the ground, which English speaking people call snow, we should have trouble thinking about it; or if such a phenomenon did not lie within our experience, as it did not for the Aztecs, we should have no word for it.

We are more likely to think about things we have experienced and for which we have names; therefore, naming would seem to be essential to thinking. It would follow, then, that properties of concepts depend upon the use of speech. It is only because of the word that designates the concept, and because of the habitual verbal mechanisms into which the word enters, that the concept can be *crystallized out*; and further still it can act as a permanent possibility for evoking unique aspects of our experience.

An example will make this particular point more explicit: suppose we have as many words, A,B,C,D,E, *etc*, for describing iron as that element has properties or possible uses. We could say for instance that A is hard, B is tough, C is heavy, D is malleable, and so on, but our idea of iron would still be incoherent and we should have some difficulty in evoking the hardness or malleability of iron when thinking of its weight or toughness. However, all these properties can be recalled thanks to the word 'iron'; it is a *metal* which is hard, malleable and tough. This form of analysis comes perilously near to the traditional metaphysical idea of *substance*; the idea that everything in the universe is composed of substances which have their own particular attributes. Modern philosophers, Bertrand Russell in particular, have rejected this classic formulation of substance as: 'a metaphysical mistake due to the transference to the world structure of the structure of sentences composed of subjects and predicates' (9).

The general consensus seems to be to treat such terms as linguistic symbols which summon concepts into consciousness whenever necessary. Concepts are an empirical system of mental relations between a particular class of objects and other classes; they order the complexity of our environment and make it easier to deal with. We identify objects and events by placing them into preconceived

70

categories (10). This reduces the strain on our nervous system by rendering recognition or indentification automatic and by reducing the amount of learning we have to tackle. If we did not classify or categorise automatically, we would be faced with the exhausting and complicated task or relating every item in our experience to every other item in the context of their occurrence. We would flounder in the immediate concrete situation and be unable to interpret it, and the prerequisite for communication would not exist. As a prelude to communication we must conceptualise and categorise.

In much the same way the librarian must classify the materials in his library as a prerequisite to their exploitation by the user. Classification and communication are interdependent activities. We have then an array of interdependent and interrelated entities: SENSE IMPRESSIONS, INFORMATION CLASSIFICATION, KNOWLEDGE and CONCEPTS. In the last chapter we discussed some of the opposing viewpoints on how man obtained his store of knowledge. Another important figure in this context is Immanuel Kant (10), the eighteenth century German philosopher. He rejected the idea that knowledge is merely the imprint of sense impressions on the passive mind. Our thinking processes are the result of the mind actively selecting and organizing its own experience. He showed that we are constrained to see and classify it into what he called categories and that human knowledge is formed by interaction with the environment. This is closely related to what Lenin called the 'dialectical element in knowledge': the recognition that what we see depends on what we are looking for, upon our interests, and on our previous knowledge and experience. The important point that emerges from this is that knowledge of any entity is not merely a descriptive reading of what it is in isolation, but rather an awareness of its relationships with other entities.

Further still these relationships are only valid for a certain point in time; they may, and usually do, change. There is an important implication here for the librarian as an organizer of recorded knowledge; he has perforce to place related fields of knowledge apart from each other and his true professional skill is brought to bear in showing the manifold relationships between them. Library shelves can show a two-dimensional relationship only. The same problem occurs with the human concept system for the psychologist holds that concepts cannot exist in isolation. Jerome Bruner (11) defines a concept as 'a sign significate network of references', the

71

sign relating to the word which designates it and the network emphasizing the fact that our knowledge is a complicated inter-relationship of concepts rather than a series of pigeonholes, and that these networks change with each new perception.

The word as verbal symbol acts as a cue; to think of one concept is necessarily to think of others. This is what happens when two people in conversation use the same cue which triggers off different associations for each, and this danger has to be corrected by fixing rules such as a frame of reference for the conduct of the discourse. We have only to leaf through a dictionary to find bibliographical support for this fact. We search for a definition of one word and we find references to many more, which in their turn refer to more words still. This problem has beset traditional classification chiefly because it has been so strongly influenced by traditional logic that is, concerned with *entities* rather than *relations*. But, in fact, the reader has his own private classification scheme; his conceptual thought forms an immense network each strand of which consists of a particular concept, and traditional methods of information retrieval have ignored this psychological fact.

Two important points emerge from the foregoing: firstly, the problem for the librarian as classifier is not so much the concepts themselves but the relationships existing between them. Secondly, the user may have his own private classification of a subject which may be validly different from that of the librarian and his storage system. The user is an information system in his own right, with his own private network of concepts and his own private classification of reality. This is a communication problem which lies at the very root of information storage and retrieval.

3.2 ATTITUDE STRUCTURE
AND THE INTERPERSONAL COMMUNICATION

We have dealt in the foregoing section with the formation of the concept system of the individual and how it may facilitate or impede the inter-personal communication system. But discussion of this area logically leads to the effects of differing concept formations and the resultant frameworks of action and perception: a phenomenon which the psychologist calls 'attitude structure'. It is a term by no means unknown in the literature of library science. We talk of the attitude of the library staff towards the public; the attitude of the reader towards the librarian; we categorise people as having a favourable attitude, and so on. The term is normally used to denote a learned predisposition, in a group or in an individual, to evaluate a class of objects in a certain way. Historically the term has had a varied career: it is derived from the Latin *aptus*, giving the connotation of fitness or suitability; it has been used in art criticism to describe a posture of the body in painting and sculpture. From this the term gradually became used to refer to postures of the body suitable for certain attitudes and this strand of meaning was finally taken up by the early experimental psychologists to describe the various forms of muscular preparedness or *set*. Since the early behaviourists such as J B Watson (12) saw mental states largely in terms of muscular readiness the term acquired the connotation of a *pre-disposition to respond in a particular way to an external stimulus*. The term is used extensively by F H Allport (13) as an intervening variable mediating between stimulus and response in order to cope with the extreme complexity of human behaviour. When Mr A meets Miss B a stimulus response relationship is set up:

Mr A	'Hello'.
Miss B	'Hello'.
Mr	'What time is the next lecture?'
Miss B	'Two o'clock.'
Mr A	'Thanks'.
Miss B	'You're welcome'.

On the face of it it looks a string of simple S-R units, the response of each of the interlocutors being elicited by the stimulus of the other. However, there may be other complex overtones not made evident by a behaviouristic analysis: she may say 'You're welcome' with a sexy smile or a frosty stare, depending whether or not she finds Mr A to be a congenial person. All these private processes or latent meanings are described as 'intervening variables'; not a wholly satisfactory analysis and one which has been scathingly attacked by Koestler (14), and by Chomsky (15). The other major connotations of the term 'attitude' is the one most used by Gestalt psychologists to signify a particular view of the world, or the way in which we organize our perceptual processes.

The attitude of the source may affect the communication act in at least three ways. Firstly, he may have a negative attitude towards himself; he may be afraid to ask a senior colleague for advice on the techniques or skills of a particular task performance. Or the reader may feel his request to be so trivial and unimportant as not to warrant the instrusion on the time of an obviously busy librarian. This is why the personality of the librarian is of such importance. He should give a favourable feedback to the reader, helping to enhance his self esteem and provide a setting for interpersonal communication. Secondly, the source may have a negative or hostile attitude towards the receiver, thereby adversely affecting what he says and how he says it. We tend to communicate badly with people whom we dislike: a salutary point for the librarian-reader relationship. Thirdly, his attitude towards the message is a factor of such importance that industrial concerns insist that salesmen must *believe* in their product and proselytise with the zeal of the missionaries of old. This problem is often borne out in teaching, when students detect a lack of confidence in the teacher or a lack of conviction in what he teaches.

3.3 PROBLEMS OF THE CULTURAL CONTEXT

No source communicates as a free agent without being influenced by his position in the cultural system. This social fact is an important variable when discussing the efficiency of communication models. When we analyse the problems of the dyadic, or two-person communication situation, such as Source A communicating with Receiver B, we have to ask the following question: What is:

a The attitude of the source to the message?
b The attitude of the source to the receiver?
c The attitude of the receiver to the source?
d The attitude of the receiver to the message?

All four attitudes might be encompassed in the situation of the sergeant handing out fatigues or punishments to defaulters. Both source and receiver are bound within an established communication convention with a definite set of objectives.

People from different backgrounds communicate with each other in different ways: in the choice of words; the meanings attached to words; the purpose in communicating and the choice of channel. We have seen how Bernstein has emphasized the differences in communicative behaviour within each social class, and how such terms as 'restricted code' and 'elaborated code' have passed into the language of sociology. A communication barrier may be erected if the source has a negative attitude towards himself, as well as towards the receiver. The junior assistant may be scared of asking for a transfer to another department or the enquirer may think of himself as unimportant and of his enquiry as trivial and of no consequence to another department or the enquirer may think of himself as unimportant and of his enquiry as trivial and of no consequence amid the overwhelming atmosphere of the library. He may also see the librarian as unapproachable and superior to him in educational attainment, and as a consequence he may couch his enquiry in the most abstruse and confusing terms.

The converse of this may also happen as when a subject specialist may underrate the intellectual ability of the librarian and may mislead by oversimplification. The communication significance of attitude and social class may have an even greater point when the enquirer perceives himself to be of an inferior social status and this perception is shared by the librarian who may tend to react unfavourably to the speech patterns of a class which he considers to be lower in the social hierarchy, thus giving point to Shaw's remark that 'no Englishman can open his mouth without another Englishman despising him'.

There must be a few public library systems which have not witnessed an unedifying scene arising from this situation of attitude conflict as the enquirer over-compensates for his feelings of inferiority by a show of agression. Conversely, when the receiver holds the source in high esteem he is more likely to be critical of the message and more likely to design his own messages in terms polite and redundant. Aristotle calls this perceived characteristic of the speaker, the *ethos* (16) meaning a quality which commands respect in the listener. In more modern parlance it is sometimes termed 'prestige suggestion' and is used as a technique by advertisers who use the names of famous people as a boost for their products. We tend to be more easily influenced by a communicator who appears to be arguing from a position of authority.

Perhaps the most important and central concept in the discussion of social structure in terms of role and attitude is that it emphasizes the importance of status as a social variable in the communication act together with the related problems of role and hierarchy.

3.4 ROLE, THEORY AND INTERPERSONAL COMMUNICTION
The concept of role was originally borrowed from dramatic theory and this emphasises the debt of sociological theory to the traditional disciplines of literary and dramatic criticism. In essence, it is the study of social life from the standpoint of the roles which the parties have to play. The use of role theory to analyse behaviour is now one of the standard methods of social psychology. One justification for

75

analysing social life in terms of the roles people play is that it focuses attention on the contractual basis that underlies social interaction and, *a fortiori*, of communicative interaction as well. Teacher and student, employer and employee, leader and follower, librarian and reader, derive the definiton of their roles from the existence of their opposite numbers, or as Banton (17) puts it: 'every relationship consists of a pair of roles'. When someone enters these roles he believes that such role playing will help him further his objectives whether they be egotistic or altruistic and he also has to learn the behaviour patterns ascribed to, or entailed by, the performance of that role.

The enquirer in search of information enters into a role relationship vis-a-vis the librarian. He perceives the librarian as having certain role obligations, in his case the provision of information and as having the skills necessary to that end. If the enquirer finds that the librarian does not appear to live up to the skills and obligations of his *perceived* role he may terminate the enquiry relationship. A social role, then, is the expected behaviour associated with a certain position, and the position is simply the means of labelling the specific role. A logical entailment of role is the concept of *status*. If a person has to perform a particular role then he has to be given a certain status which will allow him the necessary freedom and authority to discharge his obligations; a fact which has often been reflected in the struggle of the librarian to gain an appropriate status in the group or community in which he serves. The term *interaction* means the reciprocal process of role-taking and it differs from the action-reaction hypothesis of the behaviourist standpoint in that each communicator takes on the role of 'the other'.

The behaviourist precept asserts that all communication activities can be reduced to a linear chain of stimulus-response (S-R) units. Speech sounds are emitted as any other *bits* of behaviour and the process of conditioning which determines bits of communication behaviour is essentailly the same as the conditioning of rats and pigeons. It is assumed that such techniques as those used in animal psychology can be extrapolated to human behaviour without any serious modification. Like most schools of thought it does describe a *part* of the communication process. In many cases of interpersonal communication the sight of a pretty girl may act as a stimulus to start a conversation, but this by no means accounts for the

76

communication in the higher sense of sharing an attitude or an idea. The main fallacy in this approach of the behaviourist is that it assumes that the source is master of the situation and that both source and receiver are discrete units. What one has to emphasise in the teaching situation is that it is only for the purpose of analysis and discussion that one separates the source and the receiver. Both are involved in a process and neither is independent of the other. In calling an individual a source, one merely implies that one has stopped the dynamic at one point; rather like taking a still photograph of a continuous action. The same counts for the receiver; it is just that one uses a different cutting point. In this way the communication act is both continuous and irreversible; what is said is said and cannot be undone. As Heraclitus remarked: 'one cannot step twice into the same river', and the famous novel by Tom Wolfe (18) makes the same point. The enquirer and the librarian both engage in a process that is continuous and irreversible; both interchange positions as interrogators in order to bring the enquiry into a sharper focus. If this imaginative interchange does not occur then two abortive monologues will result.

3.5 ROLE TAKING AND EMPATHY

The main significance of role theory in interpersonal communication is what Solomon Asch (19) calls the 'inference theory of empathy'. He argues that one can observe one's own behaviour directly, and that an important aspect of this is the development of the knowledge of 'self'. On the basis of his own self knowledge, an individual makes inferences about the thoughts and feelings of others; the assumption being that man has first hand introspective knowledge of himself and second hand knowledge of others. This would seem to underscore the Delphic injunction of *'gnothe se auton'*, or know thyself, and the oft quoted couplet of Alexander Pope's in his *Essay on man*:

Know then thyself, presume not God to scan
The proper study of mankind is man.

The term empathy, which is borrowed from aesthetics, means to project one's self into a work of art as a means of artistic appreciation. The psychologist uses the term to denote an imaginative identification with another person which permits a a fuller understanding of his mental life and problems of adjustment. It is in this aspect of professional education that

77

librarianship has singularly failed; past syllabuses have made little attempt at a systematic study of reading or enquiry behaviour. Such user studies that do exist attempt to ape the methods of the physical sciences and fall into the reductionist trap of ignoring anything which is not measurable.

Empathy means understanding, not necessarily siding with; we may empathise with some one we dislike or with a formal opponent. Empathy may also be used as a strategy; we may empathise or take on the role of an opponent in a game of chess, or with an enemy in a military campaign, with the intention of defeating him by anticipating what he will do next. Daily life provides numerous instances of the changes induced in our behaviour by lack of empathy when roles are exchanged. Thus we may wait in a queue complaining about the intolerable length of time taken by the person in the telephone booth; a few minutes later, having gained possession of the booth, we mutter fiercely about the obstrusive impatience of the people waiting outside. Those students who are motorists will readily understand the problems of those two natural enemies of the modern world—the motorist and the pedestrian—and the speed with which the intolerant motorist will change to the intolerant pedestrian simply by getting out of his car.

3.6 ROLETAKING, HIERARCHIES AND COMMUNICATION

The use of the term 'role' logically entails the term status, which in turn assumes a hierarchy. The individual *qua* biological organism constitutes a nicely integrated hierarchy of molecules, cells, organs and organ systems. Inwardly he is something unique, able to transcend himself in imagination and thought, but outwardly he is an elementary unit in several social hierarchies: as deputy chief librarian, Grandmaster of a Masonic lodge, lay preacher, or as a private in the territorial army. Each role will determine what messages he communicates, how he communicates and the way in which he designs those messages; and will also determine what messages are communicated to him. The concept of hierarchy would seem to be an undisputed part of the fabric of social reality.

All modern societies, whether capitalist, socialist, communist, or a mixture of all three, are organised hierarchically from the centre outwards and from the top downwards. In modern industry, this principle of decision from the top in reinforced in its impact upon the individual by the division of labour at work, with its attendant

78

problems of communication. The student will encounter this in his library management courses. All these three elements: hierarchy, centralism and the division of labour were the intellectual staple and principle reference frame of nineteenth century biologists, and social and economic thinkers.

The social necessity of hierarchy is now under challenge in contemporary social criticism; yet from a communication standpoint it would seem to be an essence of the communication system and a guard against entropy. This would seem to imply that a society without hierarchical structures would be as chaotic as the random motion of gas molecules; but hierarchy also has a symbolic value in providing the rules for who shall communicate what, to whom, and in what manner. H J Simon (20) explains that the observed predominance of hierarchies among the complex systems presented to us by nature, is that, among all possible complex forms, hierarchies are the ones that have had most time to evolve; and concludes *that wherever there is life it must be hierarchically organized.* Ludwig von Bertalanffy (21) considers the concept of hierarchy as fundamental to his general theory of systems

We presently 'see' the universe as a tremendous hierarchy from elementary particles to atomic nuclei, to atoms, molecules, high-molecular compounds to the wealth of structures (electron and light microscopic) between molecules and cells, to cells, organisms and beyond to supra individual organizations.

Bertalanffy's major contribution to the integration of knowledge lies in his 'system theory', which views reality as a hierarchy of organized 'wholes'; not the world of physical particles governed by chance events, which was the world view of traditional science. Within the physical domain we have a chain of interdependent systems extending from the atom to the cosmic galaxies; in the social domain we have an increasing order of social complexity from individuals through families, villages, tribes, cities, nations, and international organizations; each entity contributing to the larger whole and yet retaining its own identity. It is, in fact, a new model for the universe of knowledge and one which is of profound importance for classification theory. Whereas classical science concentrated on the analysis of entities into constituent parts, general system theory concentrates on the exploration of 'wholes' and the interrelationships between them. Although von Bertalanffy's aim is to set up a theory of the interacting elements of systems, his

79

work is of importance for the theory of 'integrative levels' which is currently under investigation by such researchers in the theory of classification as Douglas Foskett, Derek Austin and other members of the Classification Research Group (22). The theory of integrative levels (23) is that the world of things evolves from the simple towards the complex by an accumulation of properties. At successive levels these aggregations reach new degrees of complexity and become new wholes with individual and unique identities. Each whole is greater than the sum of its parts and its identity is destroyed if it is 'reduced' or broken down again. This idea of a series of organized wholes of increasing complexity as

Fundamental particles
Nuclei
Atoms
Molecules
Molecular assemblages (natural objects and artifacts)
Cells
Organisms
Human beings
Human societies

offers hopes of a comprehensive formula for the location and citation order of composite subjects consisting of elements drawn from different levels. The generation of special classification schemes, and a breakaway from the subject discipline as an arbiter of the division of knowledge (a device which has been responsible for so many breakdowns in human communication) are also possible.

The social phenomenon of hierarchy not only influences the source of the communication but also the receiver; and, indeed, the content of the message that is delivered. If the source is in a superordinate position within the hierarchy his attitude to the receiver will be different from what it might be if they were both equals. The tone of the message may be curt and couched in the imperative mood, anticipating immediate compliance. When the receiver in turn communication his method of communicating may be more deferential in tone and more redundant in expression. Social groups with aims, tasks and objectives tend to be hierarchical in structure. The army is a classic example of this. The reason for this formal structure is that it makes easier the flow of information within the group; it also economizes effort by making rules as to who should communicate with whom. There is the old, and no doubt apocryphal story of the South American army which had a structure rather like a ladder laid on its side: one general for every private soldier and no gradations of rank in between. The resulting confusion could be easily imagined when an urgent message had to be transmitted and any action taken as a result. The hierarchy had too great a span and too little depth.

In any hierarchical group it is possible to distinguish between its members according to what is sometimes called their 'centrality index'. This term means that each member according to his or her status in the group has a certain number of advantages and disadvantages according to:

    a The number of communications each receives

    b The number of communications each sends to the others in the group

Normally the higher the status, the higher the centrality index. The chief librarian receives more communications than the newest junior and sends more messages to other members of staff.

Information and decision making is linked with power as well as with responsibility. It is also possible to extrude a member from a hierarchy by depriving him of information, or by cutting down the number of messages sent to him. He could then rightfully complain no one ever tells him anything. This action is rather akin to what Professor Peter calls the 'lateral arabesque' which is his term for what happens when some one is moved sideways and given a post with a high-sounding title; but one which nevertheless takes him out of the decision-making hierarchy, its attendant activities and information flow. It is up to the librarian who works in a special community to achieve a high centrality index. If we take for instance a college situation, one can gauge the impact of the librarian by measuring the number of important messages which come to him from his principal and heads of departments, and from the number of times he is consulted in the decision making in the college.

3.7 INTER-PERSONAL COMMUNICATION AND THE LIBRARIAN

Communication theorists regard the face to face communication encounter between two people as the most effective form of communication. The possibilities for instant feedback are enormous, and the possibility of misunderstanding proportionately less. This form of communication has several characteristics of which the main ones are: it is face to face; it is a two-way process; it is more readily adapted to the situation in which it occurs and it constitutes a means to an end.

For the librarian, the most complex level of communicative interaction is exemplified by the reference enquiry situation. It is complex because one person tries to describe to another what he does not know. At the extreme ends of this spectrum of variables we have two persons: the librarian and the enquirer. They may be from two different cultural backgrounds, a phenomenon not unusual in British cities, or from two different social and intellectual backgrounds—a common experience in the life of any librarian. The enquirer approaches the system because he has generalized about the role of the library and one could put his reasoning in a syllogistic form thus:

All libraries provide information
This building is a library
Therefore it will provide information

A request for a drink in a bar is based on the same form of empirical induction; but although many people may either deductively, or inductively, infer the function of a public bar, not all people are aware of the function of the public library. The fact that Mr A is hesitantly standing in the doorway of a municipal reference library is an indication of what philosophrs sometimes call 'an epistemological minimum' or, in plainer words, he is already in possession of some knowledge: *ie* the probability that the system or its intermediary may answer his request. This is in no way an attempt at pedantic derision. Librarians in charge of newspaper libraries, counsellors in citizens advice bureaux, and those in similar occupations, will testify that very often the enquirer is oblivious of the existence of a reference library or the services offered. He usually prefers to write to his favourite newspaper or ask somebody in some position he holds in high esteem. The history of question negotiation and answering has a long history ever since Socrates (24) provoked an opponent to exclaim:

How will you look for something when you don't in the least know what it is? How are you going to set up something you don't know as the object of your search? Even if you come right up against it how will you know that what you have found is the thing you did not know?

The enquirer has what D M McKay (25) calls 'a certain
82

incompleteness in his picture of the world around him'. He is aware that his concept patterns are asymmetrical, or in the terms of the psychologist, he is 'in a state of dissonance'. In developing his ideas on this subject, McKay used the cybernetic model of the organism which is not adapting fully to its environment because of defective feedback, and the effect of the information obtained is to recognize that organism's frame of reference. From the purely sociological standpoint, the reader is in the library as a result of a choice of several possible alternatives and his motivation is the image of possible satisfaction. If he is middle class and has had an eighteen-plus education, he will have behind him the image of his college library and certain insights into the value of recorded knowledge. Better still, if he happens to reside in a neighbourhood adjacent to the library, he will have a heightened sense of awareness. The motivation which brings reader and enquirer together, and the eventual solution of the enquiry, go through several complex stages.

Firstly, there is the conscious need for information as I have mentioned. Secondly, there is the conscious mental description of an ill defined area of ignorance, in which case he may chat with the librarian to sharpen the focus of his question, or establish as Malinowski (26) puts it, 'phatic communion'. This is a crucial phase of the operations where the linguistic or non-verbal behaviour may be offputting. Robert Taylor (27) using his own researches, gives five filters through which a question passes and from which the librarian selects data to aid the enquirer in his search. He lists them in order of occurence:

Subject definition
Objectives and motivation
Personal characteristics of the enquirer
Relationship of enquiry description
Anticipated or acceptable answer.

To my mind the above list is psychologically and logically confusing. Using the pivotal concepts of human communication already discussed, one might put forward the following as a discussion point:

Awareness of need This need may be, in general terms, to harmonise with the environment. The environment may be spiritual, conceptual, or real; corresponding to whether the person wishes to check on the words of the twenty third psalm, check on a mathematical formula, or to acquire some do it yourself information.

Generalization Setting this need against any other competing needs and sorting out a hierarchy of needs.

Physical encounter This will depend upon his awareness of the role and functions of the library and the librarian. This is where role analysis is of such importance. Both librarian and enquirer have dozens, if not hundreds, of preconceived expectations before they start talking. Manfred Kuhn (28) considers that each social act of encounter has three parts: anticipation; advanced role conception; and consensual termination.

Non-verbal interaction The reader responds to observed cues: engagement of the eyes, a smile or any other facial gesture which indicates a willingness to enter into the encounter.

Search for a common frame of reference The encounter is a bringing together of two concept systems; those of the enquirer and the librarian. This is where empathy is necessary on the part of the librarian to distinguish between the expressed demand and the unexpressed need.

Concept matching The matching of the concept configuration thus established with the formal concepts system of the information store; and therein lies the librarian's skill. In this action he matches the expressed enquiry with the formalized language of the retrieval system.

If we analyse this question of negotiation process in sociological terms, the enquirer has matched his need with an image he has of someone who might possibly be able to satisfy it. He might conceivably have asked the butcher or the baker. This 'image' sociologists call a stereotype, which is the world picture held by an individual or group and influences the way in which they see the role of other people.

A social role is the expected behaviour associated with a certain position; thus the position of doctor identifies a particular form of behaviour associated with the position of doctor, and he is taught this behaviour as a part of his professional training. A person's behaviour is influenced by his conception of his own role and this is usually dependent upon his culture. Men go to work, women stay at home; this kind of cultural maxim will determine the kind of education and training a child gets. Conversely, a child assimilates the norms of its culture by playing roles; as girls play mothers or nurses, and boys play dads or soldiers. These traditional conceptions of roles in our society are now very much under attack. Students will be aware of the arguments put forward by such organizations as, for example, Women's Lib.

Role-playing is an essential part of a person's professional training; this is why introductory courses in librarianship analyse the nature of the library's role in society, to identify the role played by the librarian as an individual member of a profession. Librarians have images of other librarians, and the public has an image of us; neither is flattering nor accurately reflects what we do. The term 'role' is really a shorthand way of describing social interaction; one plays a role vis-a-vis another person's role. And as Shakespeare puts it in *As you like it*, each man plays seven acts, and several roles in his life. The librarian will have role relations with readers and with fellow professionals. Each role will call forth a different way of communicating. Hierarchy plays an important part in this idea, as role assumes a position which is either higher or lower in some scale relative to another position. We tend to phrase a request more politely to a senior member of a staff than to a junior, or be more formal or informal depending upon the status of the person we are communicating with. At first sight, the problems of roles and roletaking would seem to have little application to this practice of librarianship as seen by the lay person—or indeed the student. Let us then take the underlying problems in an enquiry and see some of the factors involved:

1 The enquirer may lack knowledge of the ability and skills of the librarian; he may also be unaware of the depth and quality of the collection.

2 He may not willingly reveal his need for the information; he may be sensitive about the nature of his request.

3 He may have an unfavourable image of the librarian and avoid giving a true picture of his needs.

4 He may be unable to express in words the nature of his needs.

As we can see, these are only some of the problems which may arise in a communication encounter between a professional and a client. It is part of the student's education and training to understand some of the communication difficulties that the enquirer might experience; as well as developing the skills to assist him. It is to this end that user studies (29) have become increasingly prominent in professional practice.

Asking questions is rather like walking—something we have learned to do since infancy; in fact it comes so naturally that to undertake an enquiry into why and how we do it may seem to the student a rather odd pursuit. Yet when we do begin to think about it, we find there is something remarkable in our ability to coax information out of one another just by uttering a few words of our own. Very little investigation has been carried out in this area. We concentrate on the behaviour of the user, and on the flow of information in the organisation; yet we never seem to ask what distinguishes a question from all the other noises that a man can make on the analysis or the effects produced by the answer. In order to ask a question we have special construction: the interogative. Are you going to the library? Or again, You are going to the library? or, Going to the library? Here the inflexion of the voice gives the listener his clue that this is a question. What is even more interesting is the problem of the origin of our motivation: why do we bother to ask questions at all? Systems theory would account for this by explaining that the organism, being an open system, is always conducting an information transaction with its environment; the brain is rather like a totalisator at a race track, constantly taking bets, noting and changing the odds. The questioner's state of readiness could then be described in terms of what the theorist calls 'conditional proba-bilities'—the probability that if he wanted to perform an action x in, given circumstances, he would set about it in such a manner. Donald McKay (30) uses the analogy of the incomplete switchboard. This is a teaching metaphor which could be very illuminating in the classroom when analysing the reference library interview. He visualizes the questioner uncovering the incomplete part of his switchboard to the listener in the hope of having the switches set for him. He develops the analogy thus:

This brings out an essential presupposition behind the whole business: namely that the exposure of an incomplete or incorrectly set switchboard is normally a stimulus to action on the part of the receiver: that human beings are motivated to set one another's switches, or in more psychological terms to adjust to each other's state of readiness. Call it if you like, the filling up of another's world map.

This model fits in nicely with the sociological model of the individual gradually developing a world picture. This individual world picture must be harmonious and congruent, otherwise uncertainty and dissonance will result. The psychology of inter-personal communication is a field of research where much more work needs to be done and a field that might well be rewarding for librarianship theory and practice.

1 Jesse Shera 'The library as a social agency' *Journal of documantation 1* (11) December 1965, p 241-3.

2 David K Berlo *The process of communication* New York, Holt, Rinehart and Winston, 1960.

3 Plato *The timaeus* and *The critias.*

4 M Wertheimer *Productive thinking* New York, Harper, 1945.

5 George Berkeley *A treatise concerning the principles of human knowledge* Dublin, 1710.

6 Gaston Viaud *Intelligence: its evolution and form* London, Hutchinson, 1968.

7 Benjamin Lee Whorf 'The relation of thought and behaviour to language' in *Language thought and reality* Cambridge (Mass) MIT Press 1956.

8 Michael Polanyi *Private knowledge* London, Routledge and Kegan Paul, 1958.

9 Bertrand Russell *History of western philosophy* London, Allen and Unwin, 1961, p.602.

10 Immanuel Kant *Critique of pure reason* 1786. See also D J Foskett's essay 'Classification and communication' Science, humanism and in Libraries 1964

11 Jerome Bruner *et al Study of thinking* New York, Wiley, 1961, p. 58.

12 J B Watson 'Psychology as the behaviourist views it' *Psychological review* 20 1913, p 158-177.

13 F Allport *Pattern and growth in personality* New York, Holt, Rinehart and Winston, 1963.

14 Arthur Koestler *The ghost in the machine* London, Hutchinson, 1970.

15 Noam Chomsky *Language and mind* New York, Harcourt, Brace and World, 1968.

16 W Rhys Roberts *Rhetorica* in *The works of Aristotle* edited by W D Ross, London Oxford University Press, 1956, p. 7.

17 Michael Banton *Roles: an introduction to the study of human relations* London, Tavistock Press, 1969.

18 Tom Wolfe *You can't go home again* 1940.

19 Solomon Asch *Social psychology* Prentice Hall, 1952. There is an extensive treatment of this problem in the *American behavioural scientist* 16 (4) March-April 1974.

20 H J Simon 'The architecture of complexity' *Proceedings of the American Philosophical Society* 106 (6) Dec 1962.

21 Ludwig von Bertalanffy *General system theory* London, Allen Lane, 1968. p 25. For some diverse viewpoints on this contentious topic see the series of articles 'Are hierarchies really necessary' in *The listener* July-August 1972.

22 See his review article on the relevance to classification theory of Bertalanffy's ideas in *The journal of librarianship* 4 (3) July 1972.

23 See Derek Austin's paper 'The theory of integrative levels considered as a basis for a general classification' in the Library Association's Research Pamphlet no 1 *Classification and information control* London, 1969.

24 Plato *The meno* trans K C Guthrie, Penguin Books, 1956, p 128.

25 D M McKay 'Information analysis of questions and commands' *in* Colin Cherry ed *Information theory* London, Butterworths, 1961.

26 Bruno Malinowski *in* C K Ogden and S A Richards *The meaning of meaning* London, Routledge and Kegan Paul, 1924.

27 Robert S Taylor *Question negotiation and information seeking in libraries* Lehigh University: Center for Information Sciences, 1968.

28 Manfred Kuhn 'The interview and the professional relationship' *in* Arnold Rose *Human behaviour and social processes* Boston, Houghton Mifflin, 1962.

29 D N Wood 'User studies: a review of the literature, 1966-70' *Aslib proceedings* 23 (1) January 1971, p 11-23.

30 D M McKay 'What makes a question?' *The listener* May 5 1960, p 789.

CHAPTER 4

Non-verbal
aspects of communications

THE IMPORTANCE of non-verbal gestures and expressions, though long appreciated by writers and artists, has only recently become a subject for systematic and serious study. This chapter is devoted not only to its importance in interpersonal communication, but also is indicating the range and depth of the librarian's involvement in this the most pervasive aspect of the human communication system.

As we saw in the first chapter, communication can be approached from a variety of disciplinary perspectives; the same is true of the subject of man's non-verbal communication systems. The psychologist studies the relevance of non-verbal messages in order to solve the problems of interpersonal communication; the anthropologist studies the message systems of society as an *integrating mechanism* in the relationships of its members. There is a newcomer to the field: the ethologist, who attempts to extrapolate the results of animal behavioural studies to the problems of the human condition, by comparing the signalling systems of the animal world with that of the human species.

4.1 SOCIAL FUNCTIONS OF NON-VERBAL COMMUNICATION

When we meet a stranger we use non-verbal cues to form an impression of the kind of man he is: we observe his posture, the kind and style of the clothes he wears; his facial expression and the movements of his eyes. If he wears a uniform or some identifying clothing, we assume he plays a certain role in an organisation; and the knowledge and expectations we have of this role greatly determines *what* and *how* we communicate. We may also infer his life style or self-image from the style of clothes he wears and from the length of his hair. If we engage him in conversation, our speech is accompanied by gestures and eye movements; and we may terminate the interview by using culturally determined signals such as waving, or shaking hands. We can also get an indication of his attitude to us, and to the content of the communication, by his gestures and posture and by the intonation of his voice. The relevant point here is that during this interchange much information passes between us *without the use of words*. Another person observing the encounter might be able to infer a great deal about our attitudes and the degree of formality or informality of our relationship. Sir Arthur Conan Doyle's success with his creation, Sherlock Holmes, is largely attributable to the fact that Holmes knew how to make the most of non-verbal cues in extracting the maximum information from a particular situation. Examples abound of the inductive and deductive powers of Doyle's hero:

I have seen these symptoms before, said Holmes, throwing his cigarette on the fire. Oscillation upon the pavement always means an affaire de coeur. She would like advice but is not sure whether the matter is not too great for delicate communication. When a woman has been seriously wronged by a man she no longer oscillates, and the usual symptom is a broken bell wire. Here we may take it that there is a love matter and the maiden is not so much angry as perplexed or grieved (1).

Sir Arthur makes explicit a highly complex process which most of us go through almost without knowing we are involved. Other novelists, particularly Henry James, provide their readers with similar information about the non-verbal signals emitted by the characters they create. In the field of drama, the playwright is responsible for the script—the words to be spoken; but the meanings which these convey to the audience greatly depend upon the interpretation placed on them by the producer and the actors in developing their non-verbal accompaniment. The painter, in depicting the human form of social situations, depends in part for his success on representing these non-verbal signals as cues to the interpretation of the picture.

All the arts aspire to the status of music, at least according to Schopenhauer, and music is certainly one of the most powerful and evocative of the art forms in its ability to transcend linguistic boundaries. There are resemblances to human speech inasmuch as there is an infinitely large number of syntactic rules. Like other non-verbal modes of communication, it can vary in its importance from culture to culture, and the listeners may disagree as to what constitutes music, cacophony or just random noise.

4.2 CLASSIFICATION OF NON-VERBAL LANGUAGES

Jurgen Ruesch (2) organised non-verbal activity into three broad categories: object languages; sign languages and action languages. The study of the *object languages* deals with the communicative value of material things such as implements, clothing, buildings or any other category of artifact. *Sign languages* include all those forms of communication in which words, numbers or punctuation signs have been supplanted by gestures. These can include any range of signals from a wave to a nod, or from the tic-tac language of the bookmaker to the more systematic languages of the deaf. *Action languages* embrace the study of bodily movements which may or may not be intentional in their effect. They include such actions as walking, eating or drinking which, though they may be used to satisfy personal needs, may also constitute statements to the person who perceives them.

Again, if we view the human personality as an information system we might also arrange non-verbal languages according to the sensory modality to which they primarily appeal. Sign languages, if silently executed, are perceived exclusively by the eye; much in the same way that whistles and drum beats are perceived by the ear. Action languages may be perceived by the eye and the ear and, to a lesser degree, by the sense of touch.

Non-verbal language takes on a crucial importance when words fail. Words are very inadequate when space has to be symbolised, a point of particular relevance in teaching, where drawings or paintings are essential for, say, the comparison of a baroque cathedral with its gothic counterpart. Such non-verbal expositions are said to constitute an 'analogic' form of representation, a function often served by maps, diagrams, charts and their derivatives. Until the discovery of the first written documents, maps and buildings were our only clue to the habits and behaviour patterns of primitive man. Because of its time-enduring qualities the object as a communication medium plays an important role in such disciplines as archaeology, anthropology and pre-history; serving in many ways as the precursor of writing.

Artifacts often make it possible to reconstruct events where verbal knowledge is lacking. This re-appraisal of the object as communication medium is a reminder of the important function of the museum in conveying the non-verbal aspects of the social memory. As Hall (3) points out, non-verbal language constitutes a very important part of social control and this is exemplified in the way that buildings impose certain constraints on our behaviour; and, to a great extent, organise our world for us: a point which should need little emphasis to students of library planning. Any object may be used as a communication medium so long as the interpreter knows the key to decode it. Here again we meet the importance of culture as the system of rules for communication: the Rosetta stone, Cretan Linear B and the Mayan records, were all meaningless until scholars could re-create the culture sufficiently to read them; this same is true of artifacts. The object as a semantic unit communicates across the ages in much the same way as a book though, as we have seen, it often depends upon written records for the ability to decode it.

The object also provides insights into the way man organised his social space. Indeed, Brothwell (4) makes the point that the analysis of the material cultures of earlier peoples is the stronghold of traditional archaeology; and earlier cultures are defined on assemblages of artifacts or man-made objects which have been judged to be critical to the identity of a community at a particular time. In this sense the studies of archaeology and prehistoric art would seem to focus on the non-verbal aspects of man's culture; and in the communicative sense, of decoding how that culture developed. According to Graham Clark and Stuart Piggott (5), one of the guiding principles in archaeological analysis has been that artifacts, from the mere fact that they are cultural products, conform in general to traditional patterns; and any changes are shown as the product of an evolving social tradition. When we turn to the problems of teaching children and adults, and making them aware of their cultural heritage, we find that it is only very recently that the value of museums has been recognised in the schools curriculum; although the current preoccupation with resource centres may remedy this deficiency. The printed source has always been regarded as the primary medium, without much thought for the validity of the information contained therein, or for the use that could be made of audio-visual media.

Objects convey information in much the same way as the spoken word, just as the spoken language on radio bridges the gap of space and time. If we think in terms of accumulated information, the greater part of our knowledge of man and society is reconstructed from information coded in object language; from the earliest artifacts of primitive man, to the striated rocks resulting from glacial action which tell us of the evolution of our physical environment. What must be remembered in discussing artifacts as communication media, is the difference between *intentional* and *unintentional* communication. It is probable that the man who left food and other articles in graves never envisaged them as informational media for future generations; this point highlights a difference between information and communication.

After the evolution of these 'voices in stone', there developed the pictographic symbolism of the caves of Altamira and Lascaux which form a delicate bridge to the proto-literate societies of the Sumerian valleys. At this point, the skills and efforts of the historian, archaeologist and art historian, begin to merge into a synthesis. Into the realm of the anthropologist comes the symbolic values of other objects, such as the language of flowers and the language of leaves as the language of love. The lily, the orchid, and the rose each have their symbolic values which have overflowed into the more discerning realms of literary criticism. In Dahomey, a gift of parrots eggs was a delicate hint to an ageing king that he should commit suicide for the benefit of his people (6). In general, anthropologists consider culture as a matrix of interlocking message systems, most of these messages being of a non-verbal nature.

The prime exemplar of the 'culture is communication' school of thought is the French anthropologist, Claude Levi-Strauss (7). He considers that the primary mode of communication in society is non-verbal, and is mediated through object and action; including such activities as courtship rituals, marriage ceremonies, and the behaviour involved in eating and drinking. Heraldry is a form of communication which denoted the social status of the bearer of arms, using conventionalised objects and animals to communicate a particular effect and to serve as a rallying point for their troops.

The boundary line between object and action language is blurred when we use objects to transmit ideas across space. Smoke signals and drums might be considered as action languages and are one of the oldest known devices for sending speech signals across space. Both these media have been combined into intricate semantic systems which suited the communication needs of tribes in mountainous country; and the drum, of course, being ideally suited to a jungle environment. Other and more recent examples are the

93

signal systems of navies and merchant marines which employ an international code of symbols; and, on the field of battle, we note the communicative values of the standard and the bugle call. In the Oresteian trilogy we read of Clytemnestra watching for the signal fires announcing the fall of Troy; and the Boy Scout movement is indebted to the signalling system of the North American Indians—a system so elaborate that it could transcend tribal linguistic boundaries (8).

With babies, communication by object is one of the most formative methods of contact in their cognitive and emotional development. It is also an integral part of the play pattern, as when a child takes a toy to be inspected by the mother. Indeed, according to Burton Jones (9), it is a common response of a young child to give a toy to a stranger, forming an essential part of the greeting pattern. It would appear that the behaviour has some significance over and above the object given and is possibly independent of the response to the giving of the object. Child psychiatrists often find it helps to begin contact with an autistic child by means of an object such as a toy, or a ball; and once the child has accepted the object, communication is judged to have started.

4.3 SIGN AND ACTION LANGUAGES

The gesture may be defined as movement of the hands and feet or other parts of the body intended to convey definite messages, even though they may contain involuntary and unintentional information of an emotional state, such as tension or anxiety. As a systematic language, gesture can be used as a communication medium wherever ordinary speech is impossible; for example, in a noisy factory, or in order to maintain secrecy. Ray Birdwhistell (10) has coined the term *kinesics* to cover the study of bodily communication, and has formed a specific vocabulary by analogy with that of linguistics. The smallest unit of perceivable action is called the *kine*, which is a gestural counterpart of the linguistic unit the *phone*. A *kineme* is a whole range of kines and is analogous to the *phoneme*. The study is divided into three areas. *Pre-kinesics* deals with the physiological pre-communicational aspects of bodily motion; *micro-kinesics* deals with the development of kines, the smallest particles of bodily motion; *social kinesics* views of the whole area of bodily behaviour in relation to human behaviour, with particular reference to cultural context. A gesture of farewell in one culture

94

may evoke a completely different response in another; which shows how the cultural context is so important in decoding the meaning of a communication act, whether it be word or gesture.

The repertoire of expressions which the human body can demonstrate is very large; all the parts of the body can be used to express emotion or release it. The foremost of these, in terms of artistic expression, is the dance; perhaps the oldest form of ritual. As an activity, it seems to be almost universal among primitive peoples, and most probably its origin was religious. Plato (11) asserts that it was developed under the tutelage of the gods; and the foremost authority in the field, Curt Sachs (12), is also prepared to vouch for its antiquity as the precursor of all other communication forms even those of stone.

Rhythmical patterns of movement, the plastic sense of space, the vivid representation of a world real and imagined, these things man creates in his own body in the dance before he uses substance and stone to give expression to his innermost thoughts.

From the goat dances in honour of Dionysius we get the dramatic from of tragedy, an embodiment of the religious impulse, and an attempt to communicate with the unseen. Ritual, as Mary Douglas (13) reminds us, is one of the most powerful and universal forms of communication; an area of immense interest to the student of symbolism, both sacred and profane, where magic and sacramental theology meet. From the gesture dance, which had its origins in India, developed the art of pantomime or 'dumb show' a theatrical convention of communication through the use of gestures and expressive actions. This started a tradition which probably found its highest expression in the art of Charlie Chaplin, Harold Lloyd and Buster Keaton.

4.4 POSTURE AND FACIAL EXPRESSION

Our posture and facial expression indicate an emotional state whether of elation, tension or anxiety. People co-operating tend to sit side by side, people competing tend to face each other. In any social encounter we make use of these techniques to influence other people, either consciously or unconsciously. Status, as is well known, is closely connected with height and distance above the person or group in the submissive position. Burns (14) quotes an account of a silent film made of managers entering offices, showing how easy it is to deduce status and seniority from their relative positions and postures.

Darwin (15) was probably the first to treat of emotional communication is a systematic way, and facial expression is the most powerful indicator of this inner state. Emotions can be expressed in broad categories but those which are similar are harder to tell apart.

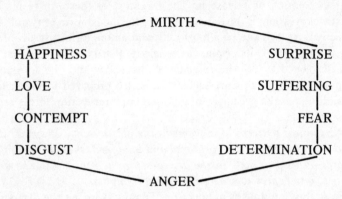

This diagram shows those which are most similar to each other and it is markedly easier to distinguish those which are further apart. The movements of the eyes perform a number of social functions in human interaction. When two people engage in conversation they look each other in the eye at intermittent intervals. We also use eye contact to initiate conversation or to forestall it; a point not without significance in the library enquiry situation which I discussed in the last chapter. The direction of the eye is closely linked to the pattern of speech: people look more while listening than while talking. Argyle (16) gives an interesting analysis of a representative instance:

When A is just about to start speaking he looks away from B. At the end of sentences and phrases he looks up briefly; at the end of the utterance he gives B a more prolonged gaze. He does not look at hesitations or pauses in the middle of sentences but only at natural breaks. B who is listening will at the same time be giving longer glances and may at the same time respond to A's short glances by signals of various kinds.

This is an important area of information-seeking behaviour, especially in the interpersonal enquiry situation, as one interlocutor scans another's face for signs of feedback. Facial expression, as evidence of a mental state, is an important area of investigation for the psychiatrist, especially in the use of non-verbal cues as indicators of breakdown and malfunction or 'communication illnesses'. Infantile autism, for example, is marked by avoidance of social contact, and recent studies have shown that one of the marked features of autistic children is their very low tolerance of eye contact. Many schizophrenics also show an extreme degree of gaze avoidance, as do depressed patients.

4.5 CULTURAL IMPLICATIONS

The language of space has been described by E T Hall (17) as the 'hidden dimension' in the way we organise reality. Every living thing has a boundary that separates it from its natural environment and, as it proceeds up the phylogenetic scale, it develops psychological as well as physical boundaries. Animal psychologists such as Lorenz (18) have shown that animals use territory as a language. Indeed, a common example of this is the family dog, who lays claim to many boundary lines within his own territory and will react in accordance with their degree of importance. In man, this sense of territory becomes highly elaborated and subtly differentiated from culture to culture.

The position of a desk within an office may have a degree of significance far beyond its physical importance, a fact not neglected by industrial psychologists, and woe betide the lecturer who trespasses on the intellectual preserves of a colleague. What may encroach on the ego boundary in one culture may pass unnoticed in another. The Arab likes to stand as closely as possible to his interlocutor, Anglo-Saxons do not. According to Hall, Germans and Americans like to delineate space by physical means. For example, they leave the room if they wish to be alone; the Englishman on the other hand uses the more subtle cues of eye disengagement and withdrawal, to delineate his own private space; probably a defence mechanism evolved as a result of having to make do with limited physical space.

Our personal orientation in space also differs from one culture to another. The Hebrew imagines himself facing East and describes West, North and South, by the expressions: behind, left and right. The Indo-European peoples picture themselves as facing North and call the hand towards the rising sun, 'the better hand' (the dextrous one). The Greeks regarded the left hand as sinister; the Etruscans on the contrary thought of themselves as facing South and the Roman augurs continued the tradition by regarding the left hand as the lucky one. Thunder on the left had quite a different significance for the Greeks and the Romans (19). Space, therefore, can be said to have an influence on people's value systems. When we speak of a person as left handed we not only mean that he uses his left hand in preference to his right but also that he is awkward, clumsy and insincere. A left handed marriage denoted a morganatic marriage stemming from the Germanic custom of giving the bride away with the left hand. The function of non-verbal communication in cultural activity has been analysed by E T Hall in his now classic work *Silent language* (20). For Hall 'culture is communication' and he labels all cultural activities by the term 'primary message systems'. There are ten separate kinds of human activity that go to make up cultural patterns; only the first primary message system (PMS) involves language, all the others are non-linguistic forms of the communication process. Since each is enmeshed with the other one can start the study of culture with any one of the ten and eventually come out with the complete picture. The primary message systems are:

1 *Interaction* It is a necessity of life to interact with the environment, beginning with the basic irritability of the most elementary life forms.

2 *Association* Inter and intra-group relationships. The pecking order which regulates group relationships. All living things arrange their lives in some sort of association. This concept relates to that of hierarchy which we discussed in chapter two.

3 *Subsistence* Like the other primary message systems, subsistence is basic and dates back to the very beginning of life. One of the first things one has to know about anything is its nutritional requirements; what it eats and how it goes about getting the food required. In human society, the satisfaction of needs like eating take on the nature of a communication ritual, having perhaps its highest point in the Christian theology of *agape*, and the sacramental breaking of bread.

4 *Bisexuality* Sexual reproduction and the differentiation of form and function along sex lines is basic to the study of culture. The act itself is surrounded by its own communication ritual and sets of non-verbal signals, which again differ along cultural lines— especially on the beliefs of regarding the roles proper to masculinity and femininity.

5 *Territoriality* This non-verbal mode is perhaps the most pervasive of all; strongly linked with the previous PMS, it underlines

the course of man's history as an attempt to wrest space from others and to defend his own. It is a category of thought so fundamental to our thinking processes, that Immanuel Kant (21) asserted that it presupposed all thinking activity. Together with time, space was 'an a priori mental intuition', a capacity basic to the definition of mind.

6 *Time* Time can speak as plainly as words. Life itself is full of cycles and rhythms, and the chrono-biologists tell us that the body has its own 'circadian rhythms' which are the prime cause of the phenomenon of jet lag. The western concept of time is often regarded as an objective reality, something fixed in nature and an almost infinitely lengthy ribbon stretching out into the future and back into the past. It is possible that this way of thinking gives us our idea of 'progress' and the pejorative term 'reactionary'. Our idealogies are based on the idea of an 'historical process'. Whether this is due to our language and its structure is still a matter of dispute. Our sophisticated urban civilization presumes that this ribbon has discrete segments which gives us the working philosophy of 'one thing at a time'. People who cannot schedule and organise time are regarded as impractical; so, therefore, we are orientated towards the future, and pre-occupied with change. This divergence of approach among cultures can be a cause of deep misunderstanding, and Hall remarks that the Navajo Indian and the European American have been trying to adjust their time concept for centuries without much success. To the old-time Navajo, time is like space: only the here and now is real; the future has no reality. One might call it a 'capsule' theory of time: an event takes place within a rigid context having no causal connexion with any other event or chain of events. The Hopi Indians reason in much the same way; there is a time for everything and everything happens in due season. Everything is relative to the observer; a fact which makes Stuart Chase (22) assure us that the Hopi language is more suitable for the exposition of the theory of relativity than the more rigid time-bound modes of the standard average European languages.

7 *Learning* Learning assumes primary importance as life tends to be an adaptive mechanism; this is really a cultural restatement of the cybernetic theory put forward in chapter one. The different ways in which people learn will still continue to be an area of investigation for some time to come and, like the other primary message systems, subject to cultural variations.

8 *Play* Play is another pattern of behaviour which is interwoven in

99

the other cultural processes. There are places and times for play, and the semantic space implied by a 'joking relationship' is a non-verbal form in its own right. The distinction between play and learning is an unhelpful one since play and learning are so closely related. The famous theory of 'homo ludens' was advanced early in this century by Johann Huizinga (23) as a basis for human behaviour. This point is not noted by Hall, nor is there any mention of Huizinga in his work.

9 *Defence* For man and animal alike defence strategies are important activities and most schoolboys are familiar with the defence devices of the various animal orders. Again play and defence are closely related: we use humour as a method of attack or defence and veterans of both World Wars can vouch for the predominance of games terminology in the more serious arts of war.

10 *Exploitation* The last primary message system is devoted to the techniques by which all organisms use their environment for survival, and covers the evolution of weapons from the stone axe to the atom bomb. In terms of the non-verbal systems which I have discussed, this section deals mainly with the material aspects of culture which forms such a large part of the universe of knowledge.

Hall's ten primary message systems are very much a personal selection of what he considers to be the most identifiable traits in a culture. They are not, on his own admission, mutually exclusive; nor are they collectively exhaustive. Culture is a process, not an array of static entities; and to use these as a classroom paradigm might be confusing to the student, unless treated as a method of cultural analysis rather than as statements of social fact.

4.6 SUMMARY

If we use the human senses as a basis for discussion we find that tactual sensitivity is probably the most primitive sensory process. It appears early in foetal life and is probably the first sensory process to become functional as the newborn child needs the maximum of physical contact with the mother. Thus he keeps warm through bodily contacts and recovers his equilibrium when disturbed through fear, cold or anger. The baby begins to communicate with himself by feeling his own body and thereby starts to establish his own body image. Later he focuses his attention upon his feet and fingers, building up visual images to reinforce his previous tactile experiences. The next stage comes when the reassuring words of the mother are used as a substitute for comforting tactile experiences.

Thus the skin would seem to be an added sensory modality, and is, in Frank's words (24), 'the envelope which contains the human organism and provides its earliest and most elemental form of communication'. The skin serves as a transmitter and receptor of messages, allowing the development of such a system as Braille; and tactilism itself forms the basis for the later use of symbols as the child learns the language of its culture. Our vocabulary is heavily influenced by tactile communication and the frequence of tactile figures of speech illustrates this. We say 'I am touched' or 'I feel', which imply a tactile as well as an emotional response. Experiences are described as 'touching', while many adjectives such as 'harsh', 'rough', 'smooth' and 'tender', are used to describe non-tactile events. Without the previous tactile experiences these terms would carry little meaning. In some interpersonal communication systems it carries more meaning than speech; as, for instance, when we console a bereaved person. Huxley puts this interrelationship thus in *After many a summer dies the swan:* The direct animal intuitions are not rendered by words; the words merely remind you of your memories of similar experiences.

The question inevitably arises regarding the interrelationships between the verbal and the non-verbal; particulary, whether language as we know it, evolved from some system of non-verbal communication. Long before the publication of Darwin's *Origin of species*, scholars had been putting forward theories designed to account for the evolution of languages from such systems as emotional cries, gestures and rhythmical chants. These theories rejoice in the names of 'pooh pooh' theory, 'yo-he-ho' theory and other fanciful appellations. Modern linguists, however, give such ideas short shrift; and a representative rejection of the evolutionary theory of language is put by J Lyons (25), Professor of linguistics at Edinburgh.

Psychologists, biologists and others might say if they wish that language must have evolved from non-verbal communication; the fact remains that there is no such evidence from language to support this belief.

This would seem to be an area where the evolutionary paradigm is not relevant, and Noam Chomsky assures us that there is no such entity as a 'primitive' language. All languages require a high degree of cultural sophistication, irrespective of whether or not they have been expressed in a written form.

Most people when introduced to the study of non-verbal communication tend to act rather in the manner of Moliere's Monsieur Jordan and find that they have been doing it all their life. Librarians are no exception. Libraries deal with books and books are mainly collections of the verbal aspects of man's reality. Yet there are several reasons why the study of non-verbal communication is important for the librarian. At the interpersonal level, the analysis of non-verbal communication is of value in the study of librarian-user interaction. The user reacts to the librarian's posture and facial expression, and decides whether he might be approachable or not. It has, therefore, a direct relevance to the practical training situation in interpersonal communication. This is an area of activity for which librarians are not famous—to put the point mildly. It would be instructive to take any library at any point in time and observe the varieties of non-verbal interaction that take place there. The topics for analysis could be placed under many headings of which the following are but a few:

Posture Do the library staff loll about, lean on bookshelves, or sit on the enquiry desk? Is there a chair at the enquiry desk for the reader? Is he or she expected to stand while the librarian assumes an unwarranted status in sitting down?

Facial expression Do the facial expressions of the staff conform to the social stereotype of librarians? Is there any eye engagement when the enquirer approaches the desk? Or is he, or she, made to stand there until the librarian finds it convenient to look up?

Space What are the uses made of the language of space? Is the library sited in a convenient position? How is the internal space allocated? Does the layout of the library say to the reader: 'Come in if you must but do not stay long?' Do the staff create a psychic space of their own by holding intimate chats at the enquiry desk while the reader desperately tries to attract their attention? These are but mundane instances, well within the experiences of any junior assistant, but they are important; and failure to observe them has led to that unfavourable image of the librarian so beloved of the mass media.

Lastly it provides a useful conceptual framework for viewing information storage, dissemination and retrieval in the widest possible context, a point not without advantage in a foundation course. During the last decade or so phrases such as multi-media

102

library, school resources centre; instructional materials centres, have found their way into library literature. The place of the book as the primary teaching instrument began to be eroded. This began to take place in educational fields and gradually the concept began to filter into the public library system. This may well have a unifying effect on the profession as the old triple alliance of 'libraries', 'museums' and 'art galleries' are welded into a coherent whole and as information content begins to take precedence over *form*. Museums have usually been considered as being on the furthest end of the spectrum from, say, the highly specialized and mechanized special library; yet as we have seen, the object and the artifact are also carriers of information. Traditional orthodox librarianship is not alone in the neglect of the non-verbal. The Department of Education and Science for England and Wales notes that it is only recently in education that the value of the museum has been realised. It goes on to lament the fact that:

Graduates in history can emerge from our schools without ever having to visit a museum as part of their course and without having their attention drawn to any other kind of evidence other than the written word (26).

Museums themselves are now becoming conscious of this growth industry and, for instance, the National Museum of Wales has made its scientific, ethnographic, and archaelogical collections available to schools. In the ideal school learning centre or resource centre there is no reason why, side by side with the books on the origin of life, there should not be found a model of the DNA molecule or a film on the hatching of larvae. There is little doubt too that the use of the object as information medium opens up a new window for the less able child. Many country library systems are turning over to the multi-media concept, and Wiltshire county library is one of the most imaginative and progressive in developing a service to education and also to the public. It is noteworthy in this respect that it includes an archaeologist as a specialist on the library staff. It is also interesting to note that E J Coates (27) defines the document, in the extended sense, as not only including the graphic and the acoustic, but also haptic records, from the Greek 'haptos' meaning anything that is felt. To bring home the point of the interrelationship and interdependence of the verbal and non-verbal universe of man we have Wiltshire country library's claim (28) that: 'A resource may be defined as any person, experience or object providing information or a stimulus to the imagination.'

This development of non-verbal media has derived a strong impetus from the transition from teacher based to resource based learning, or as L C Taylor calls it, 'independent learning'. The child's learning is not parcelled up by subjects as in the traditional curriculum. Class teaching is rare and, under the teacher's guidance, the children individually and in groups work at a wide range of activities, using all sorts of different resources: charts, slides, filmstrips, audiotapes—each medium appealing to a different sense and a different range of ability.

1 Arthur Conan Doyle 'A case of identity' in *The complete Sherlock Holmes* London, Murray

2 Jurgen Ruesch and Weldon Kees *Non-verbal communication: notes on the visual perception of human relations* Berkeley, University of California Press, 1956.

3 E.T. Hall *The hidden dimension* New York, Doubleday, 1966.

4 Don Brothwell *Scientific studies in archaeology* London, Thames and Hudson, 1969.

5 Graham Clark and Stuart Piggott *Pre-historic societies* London, Hutchinson, 1965.

6 W Hambly *Source book for African anthropology* New York, Associated Publishers, 1957.

7 Claude Levi Strauss *The savage mind* London, Weidenfeld and Nicholson, 1966.

8 Th Stern 'Whistling and drum languages an analysis of speech surrogates' *American anthropologist* 59 1957, p 487-508.

9 G Burton Jones 'Non verbal behavious in children' *in* Robert Hinde editor *Non-verbal communication* Cambridge University Press, 1972.

10 Ray Birdwhistell *Kinesics and context* London, Allen Lane, 1971.

11 Plato *The Laws* book 2.

12 Curt Sachs *History of the dance* New York, Norton, 1963.

13 Mary Douglas *Natural symbols* London, Barrie and Rockliffe, 1967.

14 T. Burns 'Non-verbal communication' in *Discovery* 35(10) 1964, p 225-37.

15 Charles Darwin *Expressions of emotions in men and animals* London Murray, 1874.

16 Michael Argyle *The psychology of interpersonal relations* London, Penguin Books, 1970, p 36.

17 E T Hall *Hidden dimension* New York, Doubleday, 1966.

18 Konrad Lorenz *Evolution and modification of behaviour* Chicago, Chicago University Press, 1965.

19 Hastings *Encyclopaedia of religion and ethics* vol 10.

20 E T Hall *The silent language* New York, Doubleday, 1959, p 88-125.

21 Immanuel Kant *Critique of pure reason* 1788.

22 Stuart Chase *Danger-men talking* New York, Parents Magazine Press, 1970.

23 Johann Huizinga *Homo ludens: a study of the play element in culture* London, Temple Smith, 1970.

24 Lawrence E Frank *Tactile communication* Genetic psychology monographs, 1957, p 209-35.

25 J Lyons 'Human language' *in* R Hinde editor *Non-verbal communication*

26 Department of education and science *Museums in education* London, HMSO, 1971, p4.

27 E J Coates *Subject catalogues: headings and structure* London, The Library Association.

28 Wiltshire County Library *Directory of resources* 1972, p i.

29 L C Taylor *Resources for learning* Penguin Books, 1972.

CHAPTER 5

Transition from
oral to alphabet cultures

5.1 OBJECTIVES
IN THE previous chapters we have examined the nature and complexities of the social communication process in the terms of the Shannon-Weaver model outlined in chapter one. I have also dealt with the problems of communicative interaction between source and receiver, both in the wider social context and in the more specific individual situation. In the next three chapters we shall attempt to treat of the cultural history of the media of communication and its value in the education of the librarian. Therefore, in terms of the communication model which takes as its components:

SOURCE   MESSAGE   CHANNEL   RECEIVER
these chapters centre their attention upon the channel and the degree to which its development influences the source, the receiver and the message. A social analysis of the development of communication is included for three reasons:

1 To show how the development of the human communication system influenced the growth and configuration of knowledge.
2 To show how the study of the social history of communications provides illuminating insights into the history of libraries and librarianship.
3 For its intrinsic importance in the understanding of social change.

5.2 CULTURAL ANALYSIS AND COMMUNICATION
A considerable body of writings exists in this very complex field, a fact which makes the design of a course for librarians so much more difficult. The growth of interest is due in no small way to the writings of Marshall McLuhan (1). To a greater degree than any other intellectual of a literary background, McLuhan captured the imagination of the 1960's appearing as the foremost interpreter of

the electronic age. But his debt to another seminal thinker goes largely unacknowledge. This scholar was Harold Adams Innis (2), a Canadian economist, who wrote extensively on the development of his native land. What is significant for the social history of libraries is that these monographs of Innis's betray in their concluding sections a search for pattern in history, particularly in the history of communications—with the emphasis on the final 's'. This latter study, which is the core of this chapter, denotes the hardware or secondary aspects of the more metaphysical term, communication. But the economist and philosopher who dealt so extensively with fur trade and fish market, and the way in which they shaped the character of the economies constructed to exploit them, not only demonstrated how the communications systems of road and rail both altered and reflected the society using them, but also developed the novel insight that systems of communications are staples, no less than the other commodities to which the term is traditionally applied.

Within this definition the alphabet, the library and other social storage systems, are part of a society's technology. Given this premise, it became possible to examine a culture not only through its economic, moral and social systems, but also through its communication media. Innis had been a student of Ezra Park at the University of Chicago, and for Park (3), technology was the main determinant of social change, including any alterations in man's cultural sensibility. McLuhan takes this thesis a step further and, for him, the social history of communications is the prime determinant in the cultural and psychological development of man.

We know that when changes in the communication media take place, the implications of what is communicated are in some way changed; and very often the substance of what is communicated is in some way altered. But for McLuhan the changes in the media not only provide more efficient storage systems and more rapid ways of diffusion, but these new media restructure man's thought processes and his views of what constitutes knowledge. Walter Ong (4), a disciple of McLuhan's puts it thus: 'The new media affect these changes not simply because they diffuse knowledge better, but because they change man's feelings for what thought, knowledge and feeling really is.'

We may not fully agree with McLuhan's view points, for communications determinism, like all other deterministic views, is

107

necessarily simplistic; but his conceptual model of the development of man's cultural history provides a useful teaching structure both for organising the material and criticizing the views of the principal thinkers in this field. Marshall McLuhan divides the history of man into three phases and each phase is characterized by a change in the predominant communications medium. He sees, as it were, three ages of man. The first one is what he calls the 'oral-aural age' where man is in a kind of Rousseau-esque state of nature. All the senses of the human body communicate harmoniously with each other. The second age is characterized by the appearance of the phonetic alphabet which disrupts this harmony of the senses and causes a break between eye and ear. This phase culminates in printing and 'printing is the extreme phase of the alphabet culture (5).' Print establishes the absolute dominance of the visual sense above all others and consolidates a sequential and logical mode of thought which is exclusively linear, resembling the lines of print on the page. On the social plane the primal social unity is disrupted and a fragmentation of society occurs. The third age, which is the contemporary scene, McLuhan calls the 'age of electric circuitry' and this age is symbolised by television. Print is no longer the primary medium and the preoccupation with abstract thought declines. The result will be a return to tribal unity, and what he calls a 'multi-sensory approach to reality.'

5.3 THE ORAL-AURAL STAGE
The oral-aural stage, or more accurately the voice-ear stage, is characterized by the oral transmission of knowledge. Sound can only travel over short distances so that although members of the tribal society are free to move as they wish they will naturally gravitate towards the centre where all the oral communication is going on. Moving outwards from this conversationally dense centre the availability of information becomes less and finally vanishes altogether.

As man is pre-eminently a social animal the sense of social space is defined by the range of collective earshot and his behaviour is conditioned by the prevailing mode of communication. Beyond this boundary is a silent and mysterious void and as man, like nature, abhors a vacuum, into this void is projected all his fears and fantasies. So began the function of myth as an attempt to place structure on this chaos. The idea of *mythos* in its Greek etymology

108

means a plot or structure and, for pre-alphabet man, it was his method of imposing structure on reality; the myth was a guide to norms of conduct, it was in fact, a social information system. Myths are similar in literary forms to tales and legends but they have a different social function. They instruct as well as amuse and they strike their roots deep into a culture, unlike the folk tale which leads a nomadic life, moving from one culture to another and passing easily through the barriers of language. As a culture develops, its myths tend to become encyclopaedic, covering that culture's view of the past and present; its relations to its gods, its neighbours and its ultimate destiny. An example of the strength of the myth as against socially accepted fact can be seen in the present Irish troubles where conflicting groups are held in the unrelenting grip of a mythological structure which defies the comprehension of a more urbanised society. However warm and comforting the interpersonal situation might be, sound is evanescent, dissolving instantly into space and, unless it be preserved in the memory of an attentive audience, is lost forever.

The oral culture depends heavily on a very fallible instrument: the memory. The problem then is: how in a preliterate society is the information store preserved? It is too much to trust to the living memory of people who will grow old and die. Nor yet again is the collective information store a passive receptacle from which experiences may be retrieved exactly as they were encoded. The problem then, is to retain the fidelity of this social transcript without suffering it to be distorted or forgotten. The answer was found in the technology of language itself, in the elaborate verbal and metrical patterns which make up the origins of poetry. These metrical patterns provided a ready made aid for the memory. In the oral culture, myth and poetry are interdependent. Proverbs are an important part of the oral tradition even in our own times: they are short, easily remembered sayings. Many of them based on the idea of antithesis and paradox as an aid to memory, and they often embody a universal principal in a concrete example. The myth appealed to the emotions rather than the reason and provided a world picture in which rational explanations were not generally called for. For example, it was commonly said that the gorge of the Peneus (6) had been created by Poseidon clearing the great mountain chain of Thessaly; in the more rational analysis of Herodotus it was merely a picturesque way of saying that the gorge had been formed by an earthquake; a solution very much like the 'cataclysmic' school of geography once popular in Europe.

As distinct from history which deals with what people happened to do *once* the myth was concerned with the *repetitive* activities of many people acting under an emotional compulsion. It provided a reservoir of social experience to be drawn on by primitive man. The main channels of this social information system were the bards, the prophets and the poets. The poet, or seer, is also a teacher who acts as a kind of polymath reference librarian; he is the man with the access points to the myth which is the tribal encyclopaedia. His own knowledge consits of the names of the gods, the tribal genealogies, and of battles lost and won. The fact that the primeval poet was the expert in information storage and retrieval may possibly account for the identification of librarianship with English literature and the 'literary gent' image of the librarian. And this may well have had a factual basis when a knowledge of literature necessarily entailed a wide general and cultural awareness which would have been of professional benefit to the librarian.

What was the oral-aural culture like in terms of social structure and cultural growth? Oral cultures necessarily give precedence to age; it is the gerontocracy who have accumulated the tribal wisdom for there is no other medium, such as print, to provide a short cut for the young. This point is of direct relevance in literacy campaigns in developing countries, where the tribal structure is disrupted and the elders of the tribe complain that they are no longer regarded as founts of wisdom by the young. In terms of social change, the oral society was largely static: individualism was regarded as an aberration, with the whole community moving forward at glacial speed. Contact with the past was mainly through the perspective of the myth.

The transmission of knowledge was interpersonal. The only way that pre-literate man could find out what he did not know was to ask someone; and the one who was asked had no records to consult. In this situation almost everything except the immediate past was a wilderness and even communally witnessed events were seen in a mythological context. Nevertheless, the social change which induced the ability to record his thoughts enabled pre-literate man to do two things: to conquer *space* and *time*.

1 *Space* Since instructions can now arrive at remote destinations in exactly the same form as they were despatched, complex

bureacratic control can now be organized and a way is made for the next development in man's cultural history: the founding of urbanized societies and large units of administration.

2 *Time* The existence of objective records makes possible the scrutiny of inherited wisdom, thought becomes externalized, and the concept of the historical fact becomes paramount as historical analysis becomes more objective.

5.4 THE ALPHABET PHASE

An oral-aural culture takes a variety of steps towards writing: stone monuments, totem designs, property marks and the various primitive types of pictography. It is essential to point out here that these steps do not mean an instantaneous leap in the recording phase of human society. These first tentative steps encoded very little and, insofar as they were not magical, they served as *aides memoires* and mere 'triggers': the information storage was in the heads of the people who used them.

True scripts go beyond these early *aide memoire* devices: a script is *an organized system of writing* (7), it is not an assortment of more or less isolated signs. Secondly, it is a system which undertakes to represent concepts rather than to picture the sensible objects around which concepts can be clustered. Opinions differ as to when man began to represent images, nor do we know when the precise boundary between primitive pictorial representation and a true script was crossed. There is still the question as to whether the primitive drawings at Altamira and Lascaux qualify as communication or as an expression of primitive magic; Herbert Read (8) inclines to the latter view. As I have pointed out, scripts came late in man's cultural evolution appearing first among urban Neolithic peoples. If one uses David Diringer as an authority, the Sumerians developed cuneiform scripts about 3,500BC; Egyptian hieroglyphics came in to use about 3,000BC; Minoan pictographs around 2,000BC and Mycenaen Linear B scripts about 1,200BC. Running parallel, in a different track, were the Indus valley scripts around 3,000 to 2,500BC and the Chinese script around 1,500BC—which was just about when the alphabet itself was developed in the Eastern Mediterranean. This is a very specialized and contentious field and any course on the social history of communications must need take note of it. But, since our emphasis is on the social and cultural factors, the minutiae of the evolution of the alphabet can be left to more advanced and specialized courses in historical bibliography.

5.5 CULTURAL FACTORS

If we conjecture that man has been on earth for 500,000 years or more (9), the development of a script must have been a novel and wondrous experience for him as, indeed, it is to modern historians who see it as a taking off point for the 'information explosion'.

Man has lived the greater part of his existence upon earth, which is today estimated at having lasted between 6,000 and 1 million years, as a 'savage'. It is only in the comparatively recent blossoming of civilizations in the last 6,000 years that the various procedures of dictating and preserving graphic annotations were invented; the art which made man aware for the first time of the philosophical contemporaneity of all human evolutions (10).

Realization of the singular importance of writing seems to have been alive in prehistoric times as well. Its origins were considered to be divine or mythological. The Babylonian *Nebo*, and the Egyptian *Thoth*, were scribe gods, and the Jews considered the text of the tablet given to Moses as Divine writing, as opposed to the human writing mentioned by Isaiah. The traditional account of the evolution of writing is the development of mnemotechnic devices evolving for both Babylonians and Egyptians (11). The Egyptian pictograph, at first, described but did no more. The next step came when the pictograph became the ideograph, which conveyed an idea or meaning other than the thing depicted. For example, the picture of a whip mean 'to rule', and a picture of the sun meant day, or time the abstract sense. In the next stage, the phonogram represented the spoken sound, with the pictographic symbol taking a particular sound meaning; although the pictorial meaning may have been different. Examples of this *acrophonic* method abound; for example, the pictures of a bee and a leaf forming the word 'belief'.

Until recently, it was firmly held that all writing, without exception, evolved from the pictorial representation of an object by a process of 'detrition'; that is, an evolution from the image to the letter. Ernest Doblhoffer casts doubts on this:

Today we are inclined to believe that the letter existed from the very outset and that the principal creators of Western writings (Anatolian, Alpine and possible Old Iberian) had already discovered the isolated sound by the time the Greeks adopted the Western alphabet bringing about a reciprocal fusion and fecundation of the

*images and the letter; a meeting of East and West of vital
importance to world history* (12).

5.6 WRITING AND SOCIAL CHANGE

In examining the social history of man and his communications
systems, two questions arise: why did the use of scripts occur in one
culture rather than in another? and was such a development a cause,
or merely an accompaniment, of social change? In examining such
an area, writing, in the true sense of the word, falls into two
categories: any design in its widest sense is either painted or incised,
and when so, apart from this design, communication is achieved by
other means. The latter is treated by the specialist as 'mnemotechnic
writing', which is the first step towards actual writing. As distinct
from a mere impulse to express an emotion, the symbols are
objectified in a semi-permanent from as a *medium* of communication.

Tallies have been used by widely scattered cultural groupings and
Herodotus (13) notes how Darius, the Persian King, presented the
Ionians with a calendar made from a strap with sixty knots. One of
the best known mnemotechnic systems of writing are the *quipus* of
the Incas, which seem to have comprised a very detailed storage
system. The *quipu* recorded numbers as knots arranged like our
decimal system. The numbers that described the life of a man in Peru
were collected as a kind of punched card system in reverse or,
viewing it in terms of modern communications, they were, in
Bronowski's phrase, a 'kind of Braille computer laid out on a piece
of string'. When a man married, the piece of string was moved to
another place in the kinship bundle and Bronowski goes on to
describe this procedure, and its function, in futuristic terms:

*The fact is that Peru was already the dreaded metropolis of the
future, the memory store by which an Empire lists the act of every
citizen, sustains him, assigns him his labours, and puts him down
impersonally as numbers* (14).

This statement is probably exaggerated for effect because what
these sticks with leather thongs could record was minimal. In fact,
for different *quipus* the Incas had to have several '*quipu* keepers' to
remember and explain to others what this or that particular *quipu*
meant; a striking testimony to the ancient lineage of the information
scientist.

5.7 ENVIRONMENTAL FACTORS

Environment can be a constraining and a furthering factor in social and technological development and if we consider writing as an extension of the technology of a culture, then the materials provided by the environment are of paramount importance. It has been suggested that writing was invented in Sumer to keep tallies and accounts or make lists, and it may have been an outgrowth of the emergence of the numbering concept in man. Far from attempting to record the outpourings of the literary imagination, the use of writing seems to have been strictly utilitarian in intent, being mainly concerned with deeds of sale and land transactions. The temple was the administrative centre and those tablets stored in the temple archives were made to store economic information.

The Tigris and Euphrates delta had no source of writing materials comparable to the papyrus of Egypt. There was however an almost inexhaustible supply of alluvial clay. From the earliest times to the end of the Seleucid era (the first century BC), the enterprising and commercially-minded Mesopotamian peoples tended to use clay tablets, cylinders or prisms for all forms of recording except monumental ones, for which, either stone or metal was used. In preparation for writing, fine clay was kneaded and made into biscuits. But since moist clay was necessary, and dried quickly, it was important to write with speed and accuracy. The making of straight lines tended to pull up the clay, so a cylindrical reed stylus was stamped obliquely or perpendicularly on the tablet. Instead of drawing their lines curved or straight fashion, they were beginning to make them by pressing the wedge shaped end of the stylus into the clay and forming the required design by a group of different wedges of different kinds, sizes and thicknesses. As a medium the clay demanded a shift from pictographic patterns to formal ones and helped to bridge the gap between the picture and the word.

By 2,900BC, the form of the script and the use of the signs had been developed; and by 2,500BC, the direction of the writing and the arrangement of the signs, according to their logical position in the sentence, had already been established. These sun dried tablets could be altered easily and this danger was overcome by baking in fires which ensured permanence. When Nineveh was destroyed in 621BC, the invading Chaldeans and Medes apparently cared little for the clay tablets. They simply destroyed the palace by pushing in the walls with battering rams (15). What is important for posterity is that the collapsing walls buried the tablets, thereby helping to preserve them until their discovery by the archaeologists of the nineteenth and twentieth centuries.

If Egypt was the gift of the Nile, then it also was the donor of writing materials. The plant *cyperus papyrus*, which grew in profusion in the marshes of the Nile delta, was made into writing materials. Papyrus sheets date from the first dynasty and inscribed sheets from the fifth dynasty (2,680BC) (16). It was light and portable and this facilitated its manufacture in sheets which could be fastened together to make rolls, often of great length. As a light commodity it could be transported over wide areas, and Innis (17) is of the opinion that its portability favoured a centralized administration; a statement which, if taken to its logical conclusion, means that the speedier the medium in conquering space the more an administration tends to centralize. Brushes were made from a kind of rush and, because of their flexibility, favoured the development of a cursive style.

The study of the Egyptian papyri and the Babylonian Assyrian cuneiform completely altered the historical perspective of the nineteenth century. Until this period, Western civilization was considered to have begun with Greece and Rome. Now, the decipherment of Egyptian and other Near Eastern texts not only revealed millennia of history, but dealt a crushing blow to theology. If Noah's flood was only a late Hebrew copy of some Babylonian deluge, what could one accept in sacred scripture? Together with this was the realisation of the indebtedness of the 'Chosen People' to their heathen neighbours. If ever there was an example of communications media altering the structure of human knowledge, this was one.

5.8 WRITING AND SOCIAL STRUCTURE

The need for records was itself an indication of the new complexity of human civilization, and this poses the problem of the interrelationships between recorded thought and the development of urbanisation. The term 'urban revolution' was first used by Gordon Childe (18) to describe the process by which pre-literate living in villages came to form larger and more complex societies. This process seems to have occurred independently and at several times in different parts of the world: in the Mesopotamian valley; in Egypt; in the Indus valley and in Central America. Childe was heavily indebted to the work of the anthropologist Lewis Henry Morgan who

115

indebted to the work of the anthropologist Lewis Henry Morgan who asserted that the mark of having achieved civilization was a phonetic alphabet or an equivalent hieroglyphic writing. The effect of this revolution was to bring in a new set of social and economic institutions; an advance which Engels regarded as being of equal importance in the history of man with the food producing revolution and the industrial revolution.

In essence then, the Morgan-Childe hypothesis is that cities come into being only after techniques for preparing coded records have been employed. But this basic criterion for deciding the transition from pre-historic town to primitive city is extremely sensitive to archaeological evidence and is at present open to conflicting viewpoints. Gideon Sjoberg (19) accepts Childe's modification of Morgan's original thesis, contending that writing could be regarded as an axis of change accompanying the introduction of urbanisation, rather than the result of a linear cause and effect situation. One of the problems is the linkage of the two concepts: urbanisation and civilisation. To Bagby (20), civilisation is the kind of culture found in cities; and for him, cities are 'agglomerations of dwellings whose inhabitants are not engaged in producing food'. Robert Redfield (21) regards the distinguishing mark as the formation of administrative elites and the consequent growth of specialized roles. Most of the specialists in this fast growing field of urban studies provide hypotheses which in some way throw light on the social origins of librarianship. A city must live on the base or hinterland of a rich agricultural surplus; it is not merely the chance throwing together of a large number of people. The concept of urbanisation implies organisation, a flow of information based upon a chain of command, and a specialised division of labour.

In the development of early cities, roads and highways are just as important as literacy. Babylon had its highways and postal services which used the banks of the irrigation canals to carry messages from one administrative centre to another. Each city had its tutelary deity, with the king and priests acting as intermediaries and the temples acting as administrative and business centres, as well as places of worship. The earliest examples of writing deal with temple accounts and it seems likely, from available evidence, that the need for such a system arose from the exigencies of administration.

These proto-libraries arose from the storage and retrieval needs of these urban centres. Here the communications approach to urbanisation provides us with a fascinating viewpoint as well as a problem for classroom discussion. If we view the city as a complex living information system, and the information context as the sum of the skills and messages available, then the library as a storage centre acts as a channel. So also do the physical transport systems which carry the messages to and from the city; or in technical terms, the sensory input and output.

This flow of information needs a technology to support it. The technique of writing assumes not only a sophisticated and lettered elite but also a complex technology: a point which is often neglected in discussing the interaction between the library and society. Technology and power, though not alone in stimulating urbanisation, are crucial variables in accounting for the origin and proliferation of cities in the ancient world. Technology had to develop before inhospitable regions could be sufficiently tamed for the growth of cities. In turn, the cities as information centres acted as stimuli for further technical innovation. The increased efficiency of iron implements augmented the agricultural surplus which released a section of the community from subsistence farming. The use of iron-wheeled vehicles facilitated the shipment of food and merchandise, and provided channels of communication for the cities which could now be built in regions formerly unsuited for urban settlement.

Gordon Childe (22) observed that cities expanded in the first five centuries of the Iron Age at a greater rate than they had expanded in the previous fifteen centuries of the Bronze Age. The point here, in McLuhan's terms, is that these technological implements and vehicles are communications media in much the same way that radio and television are; they are extensions of man's muscles and senses and they help him in providing and imposing order on his environment. The relevance of technology in the history of early libraries is put cogently by Gideon Sjoberg:

As a result of a variety of iron age implements communication improved rapidly. Papyrus, an early bronze age creation, was used more freely after the start of the iron age and later centuries witnessed the development and spread of the alphabet, parchment, paper-making and finally printing (23).

The growth of technology expedited the advent and dissemination of the document; a pattern which was to become a feature of librarianship in the twentieth century AD. It put the primitive city

117

within a spacetime framework, which imposed a pattern of order on the amount of information available. In Egypt, the sense of time beyond the grave made them elaborate their pictographic script and provided an incentive for its development; the more lengthy the deeds of a king, the more alaborate the script necessary to offer them as proof for his deification in the next world.

The existence of the library was a logical extension of the development of writing and the proto-librarian was a member of a skilled elite. As the written word was considered divine in its origins, it was natural that the temple should be its place of storage and that the librarian should be one of the priestly elite and, in Babylonia, a member of the school of scribes. Despite any religious beginnings, the records of the Babylonian-Assyrian culture were mainly of an administrative and commercial nature.

5.9 SOCIAL FACTORS IN THE GROWTH OF PROTO-LIBRARIES

If one defines history as that period when man first used graphic records, then libraries and history are coeval and inter-dependent. Once man uses an object to externalise his memory, then the arrangement of these records becomes a necessary and logical extension of their storage. Therefore, the relationship between libraries and cultural growth raises some interesting problems: Did man's cultural advance come as a product of the knowledge preserved in the form of libraries? Or were libraries a mere by-product of the growth of a complex urbanised culture? Interesting though these questions are, one must be cautious in framing the question in order not to give the impression of a linear cause and effect sequence. Perhaps Toynbee's idea of 'challenge and response' is more fitting as a mode of analysis. A problem is raised, in this case the need to preserve a communal memory, and the response is to organize the artifacts which have been coded to preserve it. In fact, the library was the response to a growing complexity; in this case by an administrative elite, who wished to organise and control the records of taxes and legal accounts, so necessary once business arrangements go beyond the stage of simple barter. These proto-libraries were government libraries used in a social chain of command. Only at a later stage would the idea develop of hoarding human thought to act as a catalyst in stimulating man's imagination and creativity. Its first phase would

118

be characterised by keeping of documents, tallies and legal records and in general to modify man's relationships to his fellows. The custom of the tribe is now written as law and this law must be expressed in written form.

It is a useful exercise at this juncture to examine the social and physical pre-requisites of the library or archive:

1 A need to record human thought most probably because the social structure has become too complex for the simple tribal system.

2 An intellectual elite with the necessary training and leisure to develop a coding system.

3 A social system of communication in a hierarchical society, with a division of labour together with a support system of physical communications which enable people to travel, and to benefit from the results of cultural borrowing or diffusion.

4 The availability of adaptable materials: the technology of librarianship.

The first two great civilizations had these pre-requisites for library development. Babylonia was the name given to the alluvial plain watered by the Tigris and the Euphrates, the southern half of which was known to classical writers as Mesopotamia. It owed its extreme fertility to the deposit of rich silt brought down from the Armenian mountains by these rivers, and its irrigation canals provided a natural mode of travel and communications. The common building material was brick, and the clay tablet was a natural extension of this vital product. The political structure was characterised by the network of city states with such famous names as Erech, Ur, Larsa and Nippur (24) and the famous Babylonian civilization, which was to form the main strand in the underlay of western civilization, was formed by the merging of Akkadian and Sumerian cultures.

The libraries were agencies to preserve information and this information was intended to ensure political continuity and stability, and to sustain the economic structure of the city. The early librarian-scribe was, presumably, an important member of this elite. Babylonia was primarily a nation of merchants, and their caravans plied along the Euphrates to Syria and Phoenicia, and along the Tigris to the Persian gulf. Any system of commerce needs a code of laws to regulate the problems of interchange; and the *stelae* of Hammurabi, which promulgated the rights and duties of the citizens, must surely have been the first instance of a mass medium. It was logical and necessary that a practical people should have developed practical subjects such as mathematics, astronomy and medicine, and should pass on the enduring bequest of the sexagesimal system.

The next stage comes when the myths are embodied as poetry, and the library of Ashur Bani Pal handed on the bequest of the Babylonian imagination in such works as the *Epic of Gilgamesh* and the *Descent of Ishtar*. Egypt developed, along the lines of the Babylonians, a ruling elite who held their power by the ability to predict floods and construct calendars; in a sense, to control space and time. Their government archives contained mainly official documents and chronologies, records of court cases and military achievements. As an earlier counterpart to the library of Ashurbanipal, at Nineveh there was the library of King Rameses II (Ozymandias) c1304-1237BC. He is said by the Greek historian, Diodorus Siculus, to have established a library of sacred literature at Thebes and to have placed over its entrance the inscription: 'Medicine for the soul' (25). The contents of this royal library are thought to have been as many as twenty thousand rolls and to have included works of fiction. What is significant for the history of our profession is that Thebes holds the tombs of two librarians: father and son, named Neb-Nufre and Nufre-Heteb. Event the most august and famous contemporary librarians of the profession might not always merit an obituary in *The times*, or in any other periodical of general interest.

Both civilizations attained imperial status; both assimilated conquered peoples and, more especially in the case of the Assyro-Babylonians, the library was often a product of the spoils of war and a medium for the integration of peoples into homogeneous cultural-pattern unit. The library can also be a weapon of tyranny as well as freedom; a cautionary reflection for the student.

5.10 CULTURAL EFFECTS: WRITING AND SOCIAL CHANGE

It is assumed by Elmer Johnson (26) that the library in Greece is a product of the sixth century BC; an assertion that is roundly citicized by Hessel (27): 'Libraries were still unknown in Greece in classical times. The tradition that in these early days Pisistratus of Athens and Polycrates of Samos had erected libraries does not deserve belief.' Yet the standard histories treat the development of written thought as though jumping like a spark from the Assyro-Babylonians or the Egyptians: the result of either copying the device itself or the idea; a phenomenon which anthropologists call 'stimulus diffusion'. The other types of linear inscription found were apparently phonetic characters and were described by Arthur Evans (28) as 'Linear A and Linear B'.

These tablets were associated with the Minoan period of Cretan history and the later period of its conquest by the Myceneans, an early Greek people. Like the records of Mesopotamia this form of writing was used almost exclusively for business subjects. By the eleventh century BC, the Minoan-Mycenaean civilization was overrun by the less civilized Dorians and during this cultural hiatus the Odyssey and the Iliad were composed and handed down as epics in the oral tradition. Then sometime prior to the seventh century BC, the Greeks obtained the alphabet from the Phoenicians and adapted it to their own language. This clearly marks a second stage in the communications explosion. The alphabet now begins to merge with a vigorous cultural tradition and its first effect was the development of abstract thought. To tribal man, feeling and thinking were identically similar sensations, and the ability of treating ideas as separate from things came late in his cultural development. Rather like the cognitive development of the child, he took a long time to distinguish himself from his environment.

Ionia, a city in Asia Minor, represents the starting point where philosophers like Thales (fl585BC) began to seek rationalist answers to questions about the universe and men (29). An inheritor of aphoristic wisdom and mythological lore, Thales represents the first attempt to explain the universe from first principles; and for him, water was the basic stuff of the universe. The teachings of Thales are known only through a vague oral tradition; but of his immediate successors, Anaximander and Anaximines, fragments remain, many of which were edited by Aristotle. From these Milesian philosophers came the notion of 'mind' or *nous* as the regulating principle of the cosmos. Man now begins to objectify his own thought processes. Then followed the philosophic tradition of Heraclitus who was obsessed by change, and Democritus of Abdera who accounted for the nature of the physical world in terms of particles which were indivisible and not subject to further alteration; a brilliant speculative leap of the imagination which would not be verified until the twentieth century.

What has come about now is a separation of the mind and external matter, and McLuhan's theory that this is the result of the alphabet is highly plausible. Once the intellect becomes accustomed to treating a series of signs as an information system independent of the thinking mind, then objective thought is a logical development. As it may be remembered, the staple of McLuhan's thesis is that the invention of writing is akin to the theological archetype of the Fall of Man, disturbing the sensory balance of pre-literate man and, because of its linear form, imprinting a linear frame on the thinking process of literate man. The time-binding effects of recorded experience had a two fold effect. Firstly, on the myth as the tribal encyclopaedia: the myth could now be checked against known facts and recorded history was born in the works of Herodotus and Thucydides. Secondly, man now began to organize his world in two separate orders of knowledge: the first which regarded myth and poetry as a separate field of experience where the statements made were not factual; the other world where statements are either verifiable or falsifiable. This is the implication of the split between the sciences and the arts. There is little doubt that the logic of Aristotle can be regarded as linear where one argument must follow from another in order to be logically valid and the influence of the document can be seen when we talk of pursuing knowledge or following an argument.

5.11 INFLUENCE ON LANGUAGE

Perhaps the greatest influence of the written word was on the growth of language itself. In order to deal with abstractions the Greek philosophers had to forge a new vocabulary and they did this in most cases by adapting current terms which had quite a restricted and concrete application. This is particularly exemplified in the formation of a new ethical language. Hammurabi had promulgated laws, but now the Greeks debated the nature of man's obligations to his fellow men and long established customs were held up to scrutiny. In heroic poetry we see how intensely preoccupying is the language of social structure. The worst and most despicable of vices are those that violate the bonds of social cohesion, such as treachery and cowardice (30). Homer abounds in moral judgments on such social

122

defects. A man was judged by the way he discharged his role; and Mycenean kings were expected to be good pirates. The term *agathos* was originally applied to the ideal Homeric nobleman, the term itself is the ancestor of our moral term for good, though such a man would not be regarded as good in conventional moral sense. The word translated as justice is 'dike' which grew into the abstract noun 'dikaiosyne', which is the term extensively discussed by Socrates in the *Republic*. The literal meaning was to denote a path or way, or the way ordinary people behave in the course of nature with no ethical overtones whatever. 'Cosmos', which now has a very abstract connotation, once denoted a woman's headress with the accompanying significance of order and harmony. Thus, once a language is committed to written form, linguistic changes inevitably occur and there is a tendency towards the creation of an abstract language necessary for the growth of scholarship.

This chapter has taken phase one of the McLuhan model and identified the main social components contributing to the growth and development of human communications systems in the ancient world. It is intended to provide the foundation concepts for a module which would introduce the student to the social history of libraries without smothering him in too much detail. One of the principal faults in courses teaching the history of libraries is that too often they tend to be a mere enumeration of events, blandly assuming that libraries originated in a social vacuum. Every student librarian should know something of the history of his profession, but the intent of this chapter is that he should see libraries as the part of the growth of a complex of social communication systems. The social structure is also a point of importance: the self-insulated elite which ruled these ancient civilizations ensured their own destruction by neglecting to diffuse the store of information in their possession. Eric de Grolier (31) has put the point more dramatically:

Now the death of a civilization can be interpreted as the death of its information mechanisms; as the death of man is established by ECG's proving the irreversible destruction of his nervous system. The civilization of the Ancient Egyptians was definitively dead when nobody could any longer read their writings; the burning of the Alexandrian library rung the knell of our 'Ancient World'.

The second pedagogic benefit which springs from adopting this approach is that it provides a gradual introduction to the concept of enumerative bibliography as a map of existing records, and of cataloguing as the channel providing a point of access. Aristotle was the first scholar-bibliophile to gather the records of his civilization for the sole purpose of criticism and scrutiny, as well as to provide a *summa* of existing knowledge. This bibliographical tradition was to be carried on in the Alexandrian libraries and later in the monasteries of Christendom. A list of important dates is appended to help in giving the chapter a more meaningful chronological framework.

Important stages in the history of communication

20,000BC	The approximate date of earliest cave paintings and the earliest expression of man's visual image of reality.
4,300BC	The gradual reclamation of the jungle swamp in the lower Tigris and Euphrates valley and the beginnings of a distinctive Sumerian civilization.
3,100-2,400BC	The beginnings of Egyptian civilization and the Sumerian city states.
3,100BC	The beginnings of cuneiform writing.
2,500BC	The date of earliest known Egyptian hieroglyphic writing and the use of papyrus.
1,800BC	Height of Babylonian culture. Extensive literature in cuneiform recorded on clay tablets; the famous law code on Hammurabi inscribed on a steale.
1,700BC	Minoans of Crete develop a script.
1,600BC	Semites develop the first real alphabet, later transmitted by the Phoenicians to the Greeks in the tenth century BC.
1,580-1,350BC	Egyptian 'Book of the Dead' oldest known papyrus —considered to be the world's first book.
800BC	Etruscans adopt the alphabet from the Greeks passing it on to the Romans.
612BC	Nineveh sacked by Medes and Chaldeans.
700BC	Emergence of the 'demotic script' in Egypt, used for non-religious writing on papyrus.
600BC	Beginning of Hellenic Science and Philosophy.
540BC	Foundation of what may have been the first public library in Athens, by Pisistratus.
350BC	All the Greek States adopt a twenty four letter alphabet.
304-300BC	Royal Alexandrian libraries founded.

100BC	Roman alphabet attains its final twenty three letter form.
48AD	Destruction of Alexandrian libraries, and again in 391AD.
150AD	Parchment folded into *pages* to make books rather than scrolls.
c3rd to 4th centuries AD	Art of reading and writing Egyptian scripts is lost.

These dates are approximate and are mainly derived from Toynbee, A *Study of history*. 2nd ed. London: Oxford University Press, 1972.

1 His major ideas are put forth in *The Gutenberg galaxy* 1962, and *Understanding media* 1964, London, Routledge and Kegan Paul.

2 Harold Adams Innin *The fur trade in Canada* Toronto, University of Toronto Press, 1956. His communication theories are developed to a major degree in *Empire and communications* University of Toronto Press, 1950.

3 Robert Ezra Park *Society* Glencoe (Illinois) Free Press, 1955.

4 Walter J Ong *In the human grain: technological culture and its effect on man* London, MacMillan, 1967, p 4.

5 Marshall McLuhan *The Gutenberg galaxy: the making of typographic man* London, Routledge and Kegan Paul, p 158.

6 Article by H J Rose *Oxford classical dictionary* edited by J Hammond, London, Oxford University Press, 1970.

7 Walter J Ong *The presence of the word* New York, Simon and Schuster, 1967, p 36.

8 Herbert Read *Art and society* 2nd ed, London, Faber, 1945, chapter 2.

9 David Diringer *Writing* London, Thames and Hudson, 1962, p 35-119.

10 Arnold Toynbee *The historian's approach to religion* London, Oxford University Press, 1956, p 3.

11 David Diringer *The alphabet: a key to the history of mankind* London, Hutchinson, 1949.

12 Ernst Doblhoffer *Voices in stone: the decipherment of ancient scripts and writings* London, Souvenir Press, 1961, p 14.

13 Herodotus *Histories* IV

14 Jacob Bronowski 'The ascent of man' in *The listener* 89 (2304) May 24 1973.

15 Wendell Johnson *History of libraries in the Western world* New York, Scarecrow Press, 1966.

16 Alexander Moret *The Nile and Egyptian civilisation* London, 1927.

17 Harold Innis *Empire and communications* Toronto, University of Toronto Press, 1950.

18 V Gordon Childe *Social evolution* London, Watts, 1963,

19 Godeon Sjoberg *The pre-industrial city* London, Collier MacMillan, 1960.

20 P Bagby *Culture and history* London, Longmans, 1958.

21 Robert Redfield *The primitive world and its transformations* New York, Cornell University Press, 1953.

22 Gordon Childe *What happened in history* Penguin Books, 1946.

23 Godeon Sjoberg *Op cit* p 66.

24 L W King *History of Babylon* London, Murray, 1910.

25 Charles L Nicholas *The Library of Ramses the Great* California, Peocock Press, 1964.

26 E Johnson *History of western libraries* New York, Scarecrow Press, 1968.

27 Alfred Hessel *History of libraries* New Brunswick: Scarecrow Press, 1955.

28 Sir Arthur Evans *Scripta minoa* 1909

29 Cornford *Before and after Socrates* Cambridge University Press, 1932.

30 A MacIntyre *History of ethics* London, MacMillan, 1970, p 65.

31 Eric de Grolier *Paper* delivered at NATO advanced Institute on Scientific Information. College of Librarianship Wales, Summer 1973.

CHAPTER 6

The typographic age and
the history of communications

THE MAIN objective of this chapter is to examine the outstanding features of the social and technological context which led to the age of printing. The previous chapter dealt with the first phase of the McLuhan model, the 'oral-aural stage', and ended with a discussion of the social effects of the development of the alphabet and their consequent implications for man's cultural development. As McLuhan sees the history of man's communication systems, the alphabet represents the serpent in the Garden of Eden, depriving man forever of the celestial pleasures of a culture which demanded the harmonious interplay of all the senses.

The invention of printing compounded this misfortune and might be compared with the 'Angel with the flaming sword' who locked the gates forever on a primitive idyllic happiness. This is a romantic view which has many counterparts in the fields of literature and political philosophy. There is little doubt that the Gutenberg era ushered in a new phase in man's relations with the knowledge system of society, and is of paramount importance in the social history of libraries and librarianship. In terms of D K Berlo's model (discussed in 1.3) this chapter centres on the interrelationships between *channel* and *receiver* and might be outlined thus:

SOURCE	MESSAGE	CHANNEL	RECEIVER
Who were the communicators? What were their intentions?	The subject content of the transmission.	The book as a medium of transfer: its effects on the source and receiver.	The audience: who were they? How did they gain access to the channel?

The four components of this model can now be seen in interaction but surrounding and influencing it is the social context; the

127

conditions leading to the growth of this new channel of communication and the way in which it might have been influenced by technological change, by social attitudes, or by religious or economic motives. These latter considerations form the subject matter of our discussion.

6.2 TECHNOLOGY AND SOCIAL CHANGE: PROBLEMS OF ANALYSIS

Like many other subjects the study of the relationship between technology and social change depends on how the questions are phrased. This is particularly true of the interrelations between technology and the growth of communication systems. Such activities are an attempt to impose a pattern upon history and much will depend on the bias of the person making the analysis. Carlyle emphasized the role of the 'Great Man' in determining the course of history, and for Karl Marx the economic factor was the overwhelming determinant. The positivist historians of the nineteenth century believed that the amassing of a large number of facts would themselves reveal laws of change. Hegel (1770-1831) viewed history as a manifestation of the dialectical movement of the World Spirit; and writers like Arnold Toynbee and Oswald Spengler attempted to show that all civilizations experience cycles of birth, growth, decay, challenge and response.

McLuhan asserts that changes in history depend upon changes in the technology of communication; each new medium imposing a pattern and constraint upon man's behaviour and shaping his view of the world. In a sense this 'communications determinism' is a disguised 'technological determinism', since in his writings he treats as a communication medium any technology which extends man's senses in any way whatsoever. There is a great danger in using the past as a laboratory, although the temptation is very seductive. The historical facts provide the body of empirical evidence against which hypotheses may be tested, but the experiments are not repeatable and different writers will select different facts and attach a varying significance to different segments of history. But of all the deterministic views of social change and its impact on librarianship, that of technological change provides material for some very fruitful hypotheses.

There are two main approaches to the topic of technology and social change. The first consists of treating a single technology as a starting point—an independent variable—and then in examining

128

the consequences that seem to flow from this innovation. One of the earliest scholars to adopt this single technology approach was William F Ogburn (1) who proposed the well-known concept of 'social lag'. He argued that technology changed society first by bringing about changes in the material culture, that is, in the material environment in which the change takes place. The 'lag' occurs while society is adjusting to the new technology. An example of this lag was the length of time taken to adapt the law of transport to the demands of the newly invented motor car in the early part of the twentieth century, and contemporary society provides many examples of the social problems of automation. Another favourite textbook example is the invention of the typewriter, to which is ascribed an enormous impact on the emancipation of women, creating for woman a new career form. One of the strongest cases for the technical determination of the social order is made by Lynn White (2). He argues that the introduction of the stirrup in eighth century Europe permitted the mounted knight to put the full weight of his body behind his lance, thus giving this class of warriors supremacy in combat.

This superiority was expressed in the formation of the feudal order in western society and existed until the invention of gunpowder destroyed its supremacy. Such viewpoints, though attractive, tend to be simplistic, and the assertion that technology Y had effect Z usually invites challenge. In answer to White's thesis, R H Hilton (3) asks why the English continued to fight on foot if mounted shock combat carried such advantages.

The second approach concentrates upon a distinct industry, making extensive use of statistical data and then extrapolating these findings to the wider social context. An example of this approach is the work of Neil Smelser (4), who examined the British cotton industry and the resulting transformation induced in the working class family structure during the period 1770-1840. Conflict tends to accelerate social change, and John Nef (5) takes the view that the troubles of the Reformation, by releasing the numbers of religious from spiritual contemplation, unleashed a large store of intelligence and ability for the single-minded pursuit of profit. Such an economic climate is necessarily a receptive one for innovation and invention, with a concomitant demand for new methods of storing and disseminating information.

6.3 SOCIAL FACTORS AND THE INVENTION OF PRINTING

Although the foregoing arguments are attractive in their implications we have to beware of imparting to technology an impetus of its own. Man's attitudes and aspirations are also important. The invention of printing was a historical event and one to which historians attribute an overwhelming significance in man's cultural development. But as we have seen in the early chapters man is a very complex being whose behaviour is difficult to predict. Therefore some of obvious questions which raise themselves are:

Why was printing invented at that particular point in time?

Why was it invented in Europe?

What was the state of the ancillary industries?

Was technology a necessary and sufficient cause with demonstrable social effects, or just a link in a chain of causes?

The facts are bare and sparse, but they are rich in their social implications. Johann Gutenberg was born in Mainz about 1400. Little or nothing is known about his early life. In 1448, after the failure of many business enterprises, he returned to his native Mainz and set himself up in co-partnership with a Johann Fust, or Faust. Fust was a rich goldsmith who obligingly furnished money to establish a printing press on which a Latin bible was printed. This bible (The Gutenberg Bible) was the first book to be printed from movable types (6). But even these facts are in dispute and there are other claimants to this distinction. The principle of printing from movable types was an obvious one; perhaps many people in different times had though of it and it would seem that Gutenberg had inherited a lengthy system of trial and error.

We know that the Chinese experimented with types made of wood and tin; yet why did they not develop printing from movable types? The technology was there, but the social motivation was not sufficient to spark off an invention with Chinese characters which were, and still are, ideograms. It was perfectly possible to cut out wooden blocks which would not be used all that often; but for the roman alphabet the letters needed constantly to be re-used and so stand up to much wear and tear.

Centuries before Gutenberg, it was believed that monks used engraved stamps to impress the capital letters at the beginning of their books. But to Gutenberg must go the credit for producing the idea of a press bearing down a sheet of paper on to a forme. In contrast to his forebears he had also many advantages. He inherited a sophisticated technology in papermaking, metallurgy and the manufacture of inks. As McMutrie (6) points out this invention satisfied two basic requirements: there was a social demand for such an invention, and the state of the ancillary technologies was adequate to make it a viable proposition.

Gutenberg was aware of the need for some way of expediting the production of copies of a book, and he set out to satisfy a growing demand with which the writing technology of the day could not cope. Like the spread of writing in the ancient world, the spread of printing is a classic example of 'cultural diffusion'. From Mainz the art of printing spread rapidly and by 1487 there were presses at work in almost every country in Europe. In 1476 William Caxton brought the craft to England to give impetus to the growing power of the English vernacular. Early German printing was in a vertically pointed Gothic, modelled on the manuscript hand used in Germany at the time, showing how a new technology is influenced by cultural values. When, however, the early printers reached Italy, they found a different manuscript hand in use. This was the 'humanistic' letter based on the Caroline script which had been developed for Charlemagne by Alcuin of York as early as the ninth century. This style forms the basis of our roman letter.

This point highlights the relationship between a new medium of communication and the one it displaces: there is always a dependency of the new on the old form just as early television relied upon the film for its content and techniques. The two forms of writing of the period, the gothic and the roman, were the formal bookhands used by professional scribes and hence, as a matter of course, were selected for the design of printing types. The third type of script, the 'chancery script', was used by the enterprising Venetian publisher, Aldus Manutius. A type representing this chancery script seemed to Aldus to be appropriate for special editions of inexpensive books in small formats. Because it so closely resembled handwriting, it could also allay the misgivings of the conservative and the reactionary whose sensibilities might be offended by the new-fangled invention of printing. Accordingly type designers laboriously cut punches for ligatures which might provide aesthetic decorations for manuscripts, but were only an encumbrance in typography (7).

In terms of our communication model, printing made the social channel of communication more effective, in that it provided aid for the distribution system. (A hard-working copyist turned out two books in less than a year; an average edition of an early printed book ranged from one hundred to two thousand copies). It was the application of the principles of mass production; it provided greater facility and speed of access. As Eisenstein puts it:

The new presses did not gradually make available to low born men what had previously been restricted to the high-born. Instead changes in mental habits entailed by access to the printed materials affected a wide social spectrum from the outset (8).

Like all mass production units it provided less aesthetic but more economically priced commodities. More cheaply printed books increased the possibilities of cross-fertilization between varied and individual intellects and, with the proliferation of this medium of information transfer, the idea of a rigid orthodox common world picture was no longer possible. New intellectual combinations and permutations could now be found and the one-dimensional view of reality which characterized the piety of the Middle Ages was shattered. In terms of transport communications, the scholar could now become a sedentary figure instead of wandering about to examine texts as was the custom in the early Middle Ages. The journeys of the monks were a part of the system of book distribution, and among scholars themselves a considerable traffic in books was inevitable; but distribution was private, each writer was his own publisher.

It was left to the growth of the medieval university to open a new chapter in the history of publishing and bookselling. The coming of paper and the increasing demand for books among the people had already given birth to another class of bookmakers; the *scriveners* and *stationarii*, the latter so called to distinguish the resident from the wandering booksellers. In Paris, which in the fourteenth century was the great bookmarket of the world, the stationers were controlled by the universities (9) and appear to have acted mainly as booklenders. Their shops were in reality circulating libraries for the scholars.

The dawn of printing brought changes to the form of the medium itself. It brought new forms of binding in the shape of paste-boards, layers of waste sheets pasted together instead of the old solid boards. The emphasis was on portability, just as the early cumbersome wireless gradually evolved into the transistorised radio. The great tomes of the old style had covers which were wooden boards often as thick as a door. The wood used was commonly beech from which we get our word 'book'. The boards were covered with leather and beautifully ornamented, but they made a book so heavy that, as Erasmus said of the *Summa* of St Thomas Quinas, 'No man could carry it about with him much less get it into his head'. The new ability to diffuse the book was eminently suitable to the theological tenets of Protestantism with its emphasis upon individual reading and was influential in the spread of the vernacular tongues which were to form the basis of European literatures.

In the centuries that followed Gutenberg, there were astonishingly few changes in his principles. Basically, paper was pressed against type and any improvements made were in the speed that this could be done. Originally the page had to be screwed down, then levers were used, and eventually mechanical methods. The first all-metal printing press was devised by Earl Stanhope, one of those polymath inventors, who could move with casual ease from canals to printing.

The Industrial Revolution gave the added power of steam to replace human effort. The rotary press was surprisingly long in being applied to letterpress work. It had been used for two centuries previously in printing fabrics, but could not be adapted for use until a form of continuous paper had been invented in the early 1800's. The production of the curved plate, cast from an impression of the type to fit on this rotary press, had to wait on the idea of the papier mache mould. The mass production of this central communications medium, the book, displays (as did the television), an initial period of slavish imitation of the medium it displaced and then accelerated efficiency, due to the collateral developments in related industries, particularly those of ink production and metallurgy.

6.4 THE PSYCHOLOGICAL EFFECTS OF THE TYPOGRAPHIC REVOLUTION

McLuhan's major work (10), which serves as a model for this chapter, views this new technology of printing with the pessimism of the romantic. His term 'galaxy' really means environment. He asserts that, like any other technology, printing created a new environment, that is it created the concept of the 'reading public'. Script and papyrus created the social environment we like to think of in relation to the empires of the ancient world but, like its successor, the manuscript technology, the means were not there to create 'publics' on a large scale. There is little doubt of its effects on vernacular cultures and it provided an added impetus to the reformation; but to assert, as McLuhan does, that it was responsible for European nationalism and the cultural fragmentation of Europe, is a simplistic fallacy. What it did do was to create a world of print in its own right, not merely as a crutch for the memory. Lewis Mumford (11) put this point, perhaps a little extravagantly:

Print made a greater impression than actual events and by centring their attention on the printed word people lost their balance between the sensuous and the intellectual, between the concrete and the abstract. To exist, was to exist in print, and the rest of the world tended to become more shadowy. Learning became book learning and the authority of books more widely diffused by printing, so that if knowledge had ampler province so did error.

McLuhan's statement that the printed word finally shifted the sensory focus from the ear to the eye has little evidence to support it. In medieval Europe he finds an oral/aural culture that remained both literate and sophisticated. The scribal culture of Europe was not one of reading, but of reading aloud. An instance of this is St Augustine's surprise at the sight of St Ambrose of Milan engaged in silent reading. His astonishment reveals the bias of the medieval world in favour of aural reading. The design of the monasteries allowed for semi-enclosure (carrells) which indicated that reading aloud required various muffling devices to prevent distraction. Reading aloud was considered to be a social act—a dialogue between author and reader. Nor was the medieval man unaware of the function of the book as a medium of information transmission. Aquinas (12) gives an example of this when he makes the medieval theologian pose the question of why Christ failed to take down his teachings himself and therefore ensure their faithful transmission. Why did he not write a book, let everybody read it and thus save everyone a lot of bother? Thomas's reply is that of the teacher—that Christ adopted the teaching procedure of close personal contact because it is the best method of teaching. Cold print separates the style from the man and great teachers convey their knowledge on a person to person level.

6.5 THE CHANNEL AND THE AUDIENCE: THE RISE OF LITERACY

We have so far neglected the component of Receiver which was included in the guiding model. What was the audience, potential

and actual, for Gutenberg's invention? As distinct from interpersonal communication the universe of print needs a special
decoding ability to break into this area of communication. If there is
no audience to decode the graphic symbols on a printed page the
most sophisticated printing techniques will be nugatory and
unavailing; nor will there be any meaningful social function for the
library. In the last chapter we stressed the growth of literacy in
Greece and its attendant consequences for western civilisation. This
tradition was taken over by Rome and, later in the Christian era it
suffered a setback owing to the turmoil of the barbarian incursions
into Europe.

It fell to the Church to become the legatee and guardian of
western culture; a role which she accepted with mixed feelings. The
Church Fathers, with a few notable exceptions, regarded the pagan
writings with distrust and acted accordingly. In 537 the Council of
Toledo ordered the bishops to open and maintain schools; but the
concept of education was restricted mainly to the education of the
clergy, and this idea was reflected in the subject strength of the
monastic libraries. The signal characteristic of the ancient library
was the papyrus roll; and of the medieval library the parchment
codex which was greatly indebted in its form to early Christianity.
Parchment came into use in the third century AD, and by the fifth
century had supplanted papyrus. This innovation coincided with the
beginnings of monasticism and the industry of copying from the
extant literature from one medium to another.

In structure, the Christian libraries copied the pagan ones and, as
in Ancient Babylon, they were housed in places of worship. Pagan
culture was in eclipse and the collections were usually formed from
the books of the Bible (the biblia sacra) and Christian apologetics.
The most powerful influence was the rise of the Benedictines whose
monastery at Monte Cassino became a famous centre of learning.
The graphic repository of the thought of western Europe was the
preserve of the monasteries and a tradition of learning developed
through such figures as Cassiodorus and the famous Isidore of
Seville, whose *Etymologiae* was the first encyclopaedic survey of
knowledge from a Christian viewpoint.

It was inevitable as graphic records increased that a synoptic view
of knowledge was needed, although it was to be many centuries
before a complete encyclopaedia would be attempted. Learning and
literacy, however, were still the preserve of an elite; most of the

population still lived on the land and extreme poverty barred the peasants from elementary education. This brings in to our discussion an added socio-economic factor; a literate public needs sufficient leisure time to learn to read, as well as the time for reading. Cipolla (13) hazards a guess that by 1000 AD, little more than two per cent of the population could read; songs, sermons and proverbs provided the main channels of accumulated wisdom. But because of the social attitudes of the era this fact may not have induced an overbearing sense of shame.

Both William the Conqueror and William Rufus were illiterate, and the military feudal class probably had a contempt for learning as an activity fit only for monks. Monastic libraries, therefore, tended to be closed systems; a fact which ultimately led to their downfall. As Galbraith (4) points out, the medieval prince did not take time to read and write because he had neither the wish nor the need. These princes had their clerks, or *mercenarrii literarii* who read for them. This is quite understandable when we realize that, unlike the modern world which is print-oriented, the medieval world was essentially governed by non-verbal modes of pomp, heraldry and liturgy.

In developing this module, the importance of the concept of urbanisation must again be emphasized: Like the Sumerian and Egyptian civilisations, the turning point in the development of western Europe was the predominance of the town over the countryside. In Marxist terms it was the next stage in the dialectic: the rise of a new society of merchants and craftsmen to replace the feudal warlords. This commercial and urban revolution was marked by a spread in the manufacture of paper. It facilitated the growth of credit through the use of documents for insurance and bills of exchange. Together with arabic numerals, it enormously enhanced the efficiency of commerce and may well have been a remote cause in the social demand for printing; one communications medium creating a demand for another to complement it.

Thus a new economic impetus was given to social change and the written word began to take precedence over the oral transaction. Education began to appeal to even the most tough-minded members of the new order as an investment, and a perjorative connotation began to be attached to illiteracy. A corollary of this development was the expansion of the universities in twelfth century Europe. Gutenberg's invention did not spring like Athene from the head of

Zeus: there was, by the fifteenth century, a pressing social demand for some method of speeding the reproduction of learning materials and the invention of printing provided the answer.

One of the most tantalising questions in the sociology of knowledge is: why did literacy develop in some countries and in some regions and not in others? The movement spread from southern Europe, presumably under the influence of the new humanism. It is also an area of speculation rife with bald assertions and unsupported hypotheses. Sir Thomas More was of the opinion that about three quarters of the population was literate; a statement challenged by Altick (15) as being much too high. Yet there was rapid growth of English as a vernacular and the Act of 1543 which forbade the unauthorised reading of the Bible must have assumed a high level of literacy among the English people, else why bother to forbid them?

The guilds also demanded that their members could read and write, and the principle of 'Benefit of clergy' provided a strong incentive when the ability to write one's name could mean the difference between a scarred thumb or the hangman's noose. This facility must have been widely availed of, as its repeal by Henry VII is a useful pointer to literacy growth within this period. Concepts of literacy have changed from the original nineteenth century idea of 'crude literacy', that is the ability to write one's name, as against 'functional literacy', which entails a higher degree of reading ability. The norms shifted as literacy became more widely available and critical standards were raised.

6.6 TECHNOLOGY AND LITERACY

The development and diffusion of technological innovation in thirteenth century Europe demanded a certain degree of literacy. An illiterate mariner could no longer cope with the complexities of open sea navigation; and in the army, the development of new techniques of gunnery required a modicum both of literacy and numeracy. These techniques were in demand as people sailed further in search of trade, or attempted conquests to consolidate their interests. As a preliminary to the later growth of science, the development of precision instruments in the medieval crafts began to debar the illiterate from participation. Lawrence Stone (16) likens the growth of literacy from the middle of the sixteenth century onwards to a 'revolution', and then speaks of a depression in educational attainment which began in the second half of the seventeenth century. This century also saw the 'scientific revolution', and it is exceedingly odd that this drive forward in the national attainment of literacy in England should have stalled at such a time.

There is little doubt that Protestantism was a powerful impetus to literacy which would seem to account for the high rate in the Low Countries and England. The Catholic Church, largely because of its conception of its teaching function or *magisterium*, tended to adopt a policy of restricted literacy. The institution played a mediatory role between the printed word and the individual which, though it made for effective social solidarity, considerably stunted the development of individual intellectual growth. The church recognised the Bible as only one of a two-fold fount to revelation; the other being the tradition of the church itself. This was mainly transmitted by liturgical practices; and, for the illiterate, by such tactile and visual aids as the rosary and the stations of the cross. There is a close comparison to be found in the Eastern 'Guru' tradition, where the books and the knowledge contained in them are channelled through the Master who interprets them. Protestantism was, in essence, a book religion in which the individual experienced directly the divine message.

Taking the problem within a global context, the western European had the greatest chance of becoming literate in the sense of acquiring a mastery of a series of phonetic symbols. Jack Goody (17) estimates that for a Chinese to become literate he would have to acquire a minimum of 3,000 characters, and with a repertoire of some 50,000 characters to be mastered, it would take about twenty years to reach full literate proficiency. China, therefore, stands as an extreme example of a culture with a script so cumbersome, that only a small and specially trained professional group can master it and partake of the literate culture. This must have had a profound effect on the social order; whereas in Europe the roman alphabet with its combinatorial facility and flexibility was more fitted for the sharing of literacy.

Granted then the superiority of the phoneme over the ideogram, why did not all the population become literate? Why was there not an immediate boom in the public libraries? The advent of printing brought with it a proliferation of private libraries and institutional collections; yet as far as the European peasant was concerned they might as well have been written in Chinese. The price of a book was

138

far and away above his means, even had he the leisure to read. Neither did the squalid hovel of the countryman provide the environment conductive to the reading act. He needed a technological environment to provide the necessary physical and intellectual incentives, and these would have to wait for the Industrial Revolution. This historical phenomenon itself would depend on the fruitful co-operation of science, technology and the entrepreneurial flair of an expanding empire. The other factor which we shall investigate again in the following chapter is that of shared rule or democracy, which of necessity entails the existence of the public library as a free access point to the cultural repertoire and as an agency in its diffusion.

6.7 PRINTING AND SCIENCE

As Colin Cherry (18) points out, the very act of writing entails a conscious intellectual effort—to write and record must make a man think critically, however little. From this medium of communication there springs a sense of enquiry; the raising of doubts and their possible solutions. There is ample evidence of a lack of enquiry among non-literate civilizations for whom things are as they are. Paul Foster refers to an African student standing on the dam at Victoria and saying: 'How odd it is that my people never wondered where this river went to' (19)

The invention of printing enabled those speculations and enquiries to be spread among a large and increasingly literate population. Now 'world pictures' could be discussed, compared, and widely criticized. Printing provided the means to record facts; and facts have to be gathered together and systematised before they can be examined and new hypotheses formed and tested. An often neglected communication ancillary, in a discussion of this kind, is the postal service which enabled scholars to communicate across distance. The public use of the postal service has very ancient origins and is well exemplified by the Roman *cursus publicus*, but its private 'person-to-person' use developed only in the seventeenth century.

Science traditionally may be taken to mean the advancement of our understanding of the way the observable world works; and the development of logical integrated and self-consistent descriptions as to why, and how, such individual happenings occur. The Dewey Decimal classification scheme places science as an antecedent of technology implying some evolutionary order. In fact the reverse may well be the case. The telescope is the product of a study of lenses by a Dutch spectacle maker, but Galileo developed it as a new technology and sold it to the merchant traders of Venice. It was obviously of economic benefit to these men, which raises the problem of economic motives and the ghost of Karl Marx in the interpretation of historical causes. Galileo also used the new telescope to study the moons of Jupiter and ultimately to provide some of the evidence for universal gravitation. This interacting spiral of reciprocity between science and technology is put thus by Hilary and Stephen Rose: 'Science and technology are interacting terms, discovery precedes invention and invention in turn pressages discovery.' (20)

One could analyse this statement in communication terms as: the interaction is only as fruitful as the strength and sensitivity of its feedback links. This feedback is assisted by a major technology, printing; and later, in the realms of the future, by the industrial library. Like printing, science was a development in the fifteenth and sixteenth centuries which followed the almost glacial pace of preceeding millennia, and it too received a tremendous push from protestantism. The take off point (to develop the analogy) is symbolised by the founding of the Royal Society in Britain in 1662. Its creation turned on two main axes: the internal logic of scientific method; and the external logic of the growth of capitalism. Thus we have an interacting spiral of economic motives: technology: science: communication systems.

Like the Italian Academia dei Lincei (1603) and the Berlin Academy of Sciences (1690), the Royal Society was an 'invisible college' and its purpose was to communicate the results of research. There was no recognised centre for a scientist to keep himself informed and one which would be disinterested: neither church nor university would be suitable for such an enterprise. In a sense, it was using a group as an agency of information transfer. Its creation brought forth the concept of the scientific periodical: the *Philosophical transactions*. This journal incorporated news of fresh discoveries, minutes of meetings and 'communication on a variety of topics'. Ziman's comments on this innovation are worthy of note by the student of librarianship: 'It is extraordinary to consider that the general form of a scientific paper has changed less in nearly three hundred years than any other class of literature except the bedroom farce' (21). One could, however, add the concepts of science themselves have undergone radical changes since then.

6.8 THE SOCIAL AND ECONOMIC BACKGROUND

Like literacy, science and technology developed more strongly in the protestant northern areas of Europe than in the areas dominated by the catholic church. Many reasons have been adduced to account for this. At the turn of the twentieth century, Max Weber took the marxist thesis back a stage further. The explanation for the origins of capitalism must inevitably deal with the process of capital accumulation itself. Weber centred his attention on the role of religion, in particular calvinistic protestantism. The calvanistic religion stressed the importance of energetic, empirical and rational conduct as a means of fulfilling 'God's will', in contrast to the more reflective piety of catholicism. Calvinism served therefore in Rose's term as: 'Ideological midwife both to the nascent entrepreneur and his sibling the scientist' (22).

This analysis was continued by Robert Merton (23) who points out that, of the original ten who constituted 'the invisible college' in 1645, only one, Scarborough, was not of protestant origin. He goes on to point out that the puritan was also subject to legal disabilities in England, which led to the growth of dissenting academies whose curricular provided a stimulus to education and the positive valuation of science.

6.9 THE IMPACT ON LIBRARIES AND LIBRARIANSHIP

The new typographic culture and the growth of science brought with it an increase in the number of graphic records: printing brought down the cost of books to one fifth of what it had previously been and a new and thriving knowledge industry had been created. This raises an interesting point for literacy, libraries and librarianship. The totality of the written expression of our culture had increased, which paradoxically made it more difficult for the individual to participate in the total cultural repertoire. This unlimited proliferation of men's ideas brought with it the problem of what we know as bibliographic control: a communication problem which was not recognised for a long time. The slow growth of enumerative bibliography in the seventeenth and eighteenth centuries meant that we had to wait until the nineteenth century systemised the book trade output, and the British Museum published a catalogue of its own holdings.

This enormous bulk of written materials contains much of what is is erroneous as well as much which is true and useful but, as Roody (24) notes, the literate culture, in contrast with the non-literate, lacks the resources of unconscious adaptation and omission. The total cultural repertoire can only grow and grow. Therefore the size of this repertoire means that what even the most learned individual can ever know is infinitesimal in comparison with that of a member of an oral culture. For instance, there are more words in the *Oxford English dictionary* than the average man will ever know; full familiarity with the totality of literate culture became impossible. Non-literate societies have, what Goody calls, 'structural amnesia' which enables them to eliminate unwanted material. It is a paradox that very often those who ardently wished to reform society considered this bulk of graphic materials to be an obstacle; others less altruistic took incendiary means to remedy this 'defect'.

Libraries in their historical development are a supreme example of cultural lag. The upheavals of the Reformation took heavy toll of the libraries of Europe and, though the monastic library enriched the estate of many a nobleman, libraries continued to be the preserve of elite, this time a secular one. Printing changed the form of the book so that instead of lying horizontally in cases (or in chains) they could be arranged vertically in cases, with a consequent influence upon library design. Balconies were constructed for easy access to the shelves and this gallery type of building became popular until the nineteenth century, when Sir Anthony Pannizzi separated books from reader in designing the reading room of the British Museum.

The first efforts to control the explosion of literature was made by the German scholar Conrad Gesner who, in 1545, founded scientific bibliography with his *Bibliotheca universalis*. The new era of intellectual activity did not seem to give libraries any new direction and purpose other than the function of conserving materials. In the sphere of librarianship the one figure who stands out is the philosopher Gottfried Leibnitz (25) who made out a case for the social function of the scholarly research library. The new scientific attitude was not, however, without influence. It is significant that the first four librarians of the British Museum were Fellows of the Royal Society, although it should be pointed out that the British Museum was less a place for study than for exhibition and, in its first phase, the natural history collections formed the more important part of its holdings.

As outlined in the beginning of the chapter, this module centres

142

round the following interlocking concepts: TECHNOLOGY: URBANIZATION: LITERACY: PRINTING: LIBRARIES.

The discussion of technological determinism helps to give us an insight into elementary historical analysis. The use of a communication model helps to bring together material that might otherwise seem diffuse and unstructured. The technological approach can be extended in the classroom as a challenge to the student to analyse the technological and economic assumptions that underlie the simplest form of library. For example it assumes, even in the crudest sense: BUILDING TECHNOLOGY: PRINTING: PAPER: BINDERIES: FINANCE.

Each of these components can be analysed into smaller entities; and the student can be shown that a library does not spring from a social vacuum, but that it is the result of a long cumulative sequence of technical, economic and social development. This links in with the question of the 'protestant ethic' as a hypothesis: the public library in particular is significantly more developed in protestant countries. In developing these concepts the model can be used for an extended exposition:

SOURCE	MESSAGE	CHANNEL	RECEIVER
Library	Subject	Books	Readers/Users
Information store	content	Journals	Who are they?

This model leads to a further discussion of social and educational factors in the growth of libraries. These discussions provide a useful foundation for later studies, particularly in comparative librarianship and the problems of communications in underdeveloped countries where literacy and technical expertise cannot be assumed as they can in advanced industrial societies. The concept of RECEIVER can then be analysed into: LITERACY: ATTITUDES: MOTIVATION: ACCESS TO THE LIBRARY: INTELLECTUAL AND SOCIAL NEEDS.

These are topics that have only recently entered into the librarian's sphere of interest. It is salutary for the beginner that he should be aware of them at the outset.

One of the secondary intentions of chapters five and six is that they should provide a communications-oriented history of library development in western Europe, as a foundation for more intensive studies if the student wishes. The following significant dates from the history of communications are suggested:

1221 Movable type made of wood appears in China.

1295 Paper introduced into Europe.

1373 Charles V opens the National Library in Paris. Now the Bibliotheque Nationale.

1452 Johann Gutenberg of Mainz invented printing from movable type.

1476 William Caxton sets up a printing press in England.

1545 Conrad Gesner founded scientific bibliography with his *Bibliotheca universalis*.

1663 Royal Society founded.

1759 British Museum opened.

1796-9 Alois Senefelder perfects the invention of lithography.

1803 Process perfected for the continuous manufacture of paper.

1814 *The times* operates the first steam-powered press producing 1,100 newsheets per hour.

1846 Richard Hoe perfects his rotary press capable of producing 8,1000 copies per hour.

1 William F Ogburn 'How technology causes social change' *in* F Allen *Technology and social change,* New York, Appleton, 1971.

2 Lynn White *Medieval technology and social change* London, Oxford University Press, 1966.

3 R H Hilton and P H Sawyer 'Technical determinism: the stirrup and the plough' in *Past and present* 24, April 1963, p 90-100.

4 Neil Smelser *Social change and the industrial revolution* Chicago, Chicago University Press, 1969.

5 John Nef *War and human progress: the rise of industrial civilization* New York, Norton, 1968.

6 D C McMurtie *The book: the story of printing and bookmaking* London, Oxford University Press, 1942, p 127-33.

7 James Moran *The printing press* London, Faber, 1972.

8 Elizabeth Eisenstein 'Some conjectures about the impact of printing on western society and thought' *Journal of modern history* 40, 1968, p 1-56.

9 Frank Mumby *History of publishing and bookselling* 2nd ed, London, Cape, 1973, p 33.

10 Marshall McLuhan *Gutenberg galaxy* 1964.

11 Lewis Mumford *Technics and civilization* New York, Harcourt, 1934, p 186.

12 Thomas Aquinas *Summa theologica* book 3.

13 Carlo M Cipolla *Literacy and development in the west* Penguin Books, 1969.

14 V H Golbraith 'The literacy of the medieval English kings' in *Proceedings of the British Academy* 21, 1935, p 201-10.

15 Richard Altick *The English common reader* Chicago, Chicago University Press, 1962, p 15.

16 Lawrence Stone 'The educational revolution in England, 1560-1640' in

Past and present 28, 1964, p 41-62.

17 Jack Goody *Literacy in traditional societies* Cambridge, Cambridge University Press, 1968.

18 Colin Cherry *World communications: threat or promise* New York, Wiley, 1970.

19 Paul Foster *White to move: portrait of East Africa today* London, Eyre and Spottiswoode, 1969.

20 Hilary and Stephen Rose *Science and society* London, Allen Lane, 1969.

21 John Ziman *Public knowledge: the social dimension of science* Cambridge, Cambridge University Press, p 102.

22 H and S Rose *Op cit* p 12.

23 Robert J Merton *Science, technology and society in seventeenth century England* New York, Harper & Row, 1970.

24 Jack Goody *Op cit*

25 Mary Newman *Lebnitz and the German library scene* London, Library Association, 1966.

CHAPTER 7

Communications
technology and society

THE PURPOSE of this chapter is to deal with the third stage in the social history of communications technology and to suggest a method which would serve to examine the basic concepts underlying modern society and contemporary librarianship. As the title of the chapter indicates the enquiry is centred round two interlocking concepts, mass society and mass communications, and the intention is to analyse the supporting social, economic and technological infrastructure which are assumed by these phenomena.

7.2 THE IDEAS OF MASS SOCIETY

The pursuit of this aim brings many intellectual difficulties as the use of the term 'mass' often tells us more about the person using the term than about the idea to which it is intended to refer. Any discussion of this area, however generalized, involves an encounter with a lengthy and complex tradition of sociological thought and our task is to select those segments which are most relevant to the social aspects of libraries and librarianship. Mass society, as a description of modern society, is a term used in any textbook which has the vaguest leanings towards societal analysis; it is also a common term in colloquial usage as may been seen from the following:

1 General descriptive terms
  Mass production
  Mass meetings
  Mass protests
  Mass movements
2 Modern communications terms
  Mass media
  Mass communications
  Mass culture
  Mass persuasion

3 Behavioural sciences
   Mass society
   Mass behaviour

It is a difficult term to pin down in a neat definition and, despite its frequent usage, we find ourselves echoing the complaint of Pooh that 'the more we search for it the more it isn't there.' Etymologically, the term comes from the Greek *maza* meaning dough or barley meal. In its simplest sense it means an aggregate of people without distinction of group or individuals, and as such it has come to characterise modern western society. The concept has an interesting and illuminating history. The idea of the undifferentiated and the many, goes back to the time of Plato where the producers (hoi polloi) were ruled by a philosophical elite. It was only after the French revolution that the term began to take on some of its modern connotations. To the aristocratic critic the term meant 'the rabble'; 'the great unwashed'; the *mobile vulgus*. It gradually came to be applied perjoratively to the new urban industrial workers uprooted from a more stable rural setting.

In contemporary usage the term designates the *kinds of relationships* that exist between members of an urban society in contrast to those obtaining between members of a folk culture. According to Kornhauser (1), mass society embraces the following characteristics:
1 Large scale industrialization and division of labour.
2 Complex bureaucratic administration.
3 Mass communication systems to act as a form of social control over a collectivity of isolated individuals.

7.3 ORIGINS OF THE IDEA

Having thus introduced this new idea to a class, further questions raise themselves. When and where did the notion of mass society originate? How did it acquire such a sinister connotation? What is its relevance to the growth of libraries? We frequently find reference in our professional press to the importance of 'mass literacy'; to the information needs of 'mass production'; and the influence on libraries of 'mass communications'. To help us we might invoke the aid of philosophical analysis.

The main characteristic of such a technique is the attempt to define a concept with reference to its opposite. For instance, a discussion on freedom must necessarily include some analysis of 'non-freedom' or tyranny. Most subject headings, lists and thesauri, which deal with so-called 'soft sciences', make some provision for these necessary linkages. The 'opposite' of mass society is traditional society. Traditional society is characterized by a rigid hierarchical structure; each member of that society having a specified role to play; a role into which he was usually born, and one in which he expected to die. This basis of such a stable society was the kinship network which ensured group loyalities and a static society.

In the past, large societies were divided into many segments, each separate and independent of the other. The important point, however, is that though a society might contain thousands of villages, it could not be called a mass society because human relations were centred on the village as a social unit. Communications were filtered down through the social hierarchy—not transmitted directly from an institutionalised centre which is an important characteristic of mass society. One might contrast India with Belgium to exemplify this point: India has a much larger population but cannot be called (at least yet) a mass society. The difference, therefore, lies not in the size of population or geographic area, but in the *communicating relationships* that exist between members of that society. One of the most famous sociologists to examine these two types of society was Emile Durkheim, who was greatly interested in the problems of social change and its psychological effects upon the individual. Durkheim (2) called the social bonds that characterised primitive society 'mechanical', that is because the people are so little differentiated and are held together by the external forces of kinship and neighbourliness. People are bound together by ties of loyalty, and face-to-face communication is paramount. This idealised construct resembles McLuhan's oral-aural stage of society.

With the advent of industrial society, man is uprooted from this comforting network and becomes incapable of relating himself effectively to others. Such a state Durkheim calls *anomie* or normlessness; a term frequently used in the analysis of contemporary social ills. Ferdinand Tonnies, the German sociologist, working on the same lines as Durkheim, puts forward two theoretical types of social organization: the first a pre-industrial society or community which he called *Gemeinschaft*; the second is the industrial society towards which a community naturally evolves, and this type he calls a *Gesellschaft* society (3).

Like Durkheim's primitive society, the members of the *Gemein-*

148

schaft or community were bound together by the reciprocal binding sentiments of religion and kinship; but this new kind of industrial society or *Gesellschaft* is based on contractual relationships, by large formal organizations, by the division of labour and by the laws of the market. The communication relationships are no longer the personal in-depth encounters of the community, but the impersonal and contractual relationships of buyer and seller, employer and employee. A man no longer makes a pair of boots, but a small part of one boot at factory bench; he no longer sees, or takes pride in, the finished product.

This then is the conceptual model of the kind of society in which mass communications developed, in which the great movements of mass literacy were initiated and in which the redoubtable Colonel Sibthorp inveighed against the evils of public education and public libraries. The concepts of mass society have their counterparts in the problems of 'mass culture' and other crises of sensibility that have occurred in the history of literary criticism. These crises were caused by the fear that the cultural heritage would be endangered once it became accessible to the 'masses'.

7.4 MASS SOCIETY AND TECHNOLOGY

But this social change, which had to exercise the minds of the nineteenth century sociologists, was in itself the result of the application of technology to economic problems. The developments in technology and science which had been stimulated by the invention of printing, had culminated in an epoch of technological innovation without precedent in man's history. This is the 'Industrial Revolution', a term with which most students should be familiar. The origins of the term is ascribed to Arnold Toynbee (1852-83), the economist and social reformer who used it to describe the sudden acceleration of technical development which took place in Europe from the late eighteenth century and which transferred the balance of political power from the landowner to the industrial capitalist, and created an industrial working class. David Landes (4) defines it as:

That complex of technical innovations which by substituting machines from human skill, and inanimate power for human and animal force brings about a shift from handicraft to manufacture; and, in so doing, gives birth to a modern economy.

Opinions differ as to the usage of the term and its historical dating. According to Landes there were several industrial revolutions in the course of man's history; there was, for instance, an 'industrial revolution' in the thirteenth century which led to the growth of medieval urbanism. But the words, when capitalized, have a different meaning. They denote *the* 'Industrial Revolution' which began in England in the eighteenth century and which represented a breakthrough from an agrarian handicraft economy to one dominated by machine manufacture. Historians such as John Nef (5) argue that this Industrial Revolution had its origins, not in the eighteenth century, but in the growth of British iron and coal industries during the relatively peaceful period from 1540 to 1640. Lewis Mumford (6) refuses to see this period as an isolated epoch, seeing the whole history of man as a continuous development in technology.

Whatever the diversity of opinion on the point, this period from the middle eighteenth century had at its heart an interrelated succession of technological changes; the principal one being the substitution of mechanical for human power, together with an improvement in the getting of raw materials—especially in what we now know as the mechanical and metallurgical industries. The importance of examining this historical concept in a course of this kind has four main reasons:

1 It brought with it an increase in political power-sharing by the 'masses'.
2 There was a rapid increase in the development of communications technology.
3 The essence of such a change made literacy essential.
4 This period saw the growth of the public library concept as a corollary to the first three.

All these factors contributed to an acceleration in the amount of available knowledge in society: this store could no longer be the preserve of either an ecclesiastical or a secular elite. Such a knowledge industry continually recreated its own momentum, culminating in what we know today as the 'information explosion'. New forms of industrialisation, with their accompanying changes in the social structure, created new problems in management and in the control and co-ordination of large groups of workers. It resulted in the eventual emergence of the concepts of 'efficiency' and in the time and motion study approach of Frederick Onslow Taylor (7). The individual was now a depersonalised unit, 'the factory hand', and this is the alienated individual spoken of by Durkheim.

The environment thus produced is that which Blake castigated, and which the central tradition of literary criticism in England has always held to be an embodiment of the archetypal 'original sin'. Karl Marx used the term 'alienation' to describe this historical condition. He argued that capitalism had reversed the relationship between men and the things they produce. Such things had ceased to be under human control and the skills of the producer are sold to the owner in return for a wage. The product becomes a commodity; it controls men and reduces them to a commodity like itself. Man is thus alienated from his world and other forms of relationships are shown to follow.

7.5 MASS SOCIETY AND COMMUNICATIONS TECHNOLOGY

This was the kind of society in which origins of mass communications took place. As we noted with regard to the invention of printing, technical improvements are feasible only after advances in associated fields. The steam engine is a classic example of what Landes (8) calls 'technological interrelatedness'. It was impossible to produce an effective condensing engine until better methods of metal-working could turn out accurate cylinders. The demand for coal, pushed mines deeper until water seepage became a dangerous hazard: the answer was the creation of a more efficient pump, the steam engine. What is important here is the economic value system which is always on the alert for any innovation which assists in the increase in productivity. It is the kind of mentality which Koestler (9) calls 'bisociation', that is the ability to transfer an innovation to another frame of reference which has no obvious connexion.

Steam was transferred to transport problems and to the speeding up of the printing process which was to make newspapers and books cheaper and thereby enhance the opportunities of mass literacy and political involvement. New industrial developments brought with them new problems in communication, and more important still, the economic motivation to solve them. This economic factor is of immense importance in examining the interrelationships between technology and the advance in communications. As we saw with the invention of the steam engine the ultimate application of an invention is not always the original one conceived in the mind of the inventor. Very often innovation is a 'spin-off' from the original process. An example of this was Perkin's discovery in 1856 of the

151

first synthetic aniline dye. Although he made the discovery while attempting to synthesise quinine, Perkin immediately realized the economic usefulness of the dye which had stained the cloth on his laboratory table. As Daniels (10) shows the long existing demands for new and cheaper sources of dyes facilitated Perkin's transfer from invention to successful innovation.

For all we know, Gutenberg may have been trying to perfect the wine press of his day and the printing press may have been an idea which occurred to him while so doing. Whatever his intentions the art of printing brought forth another, perhaps more powerful, medium of communication and the oldest of the mass media. Newspapers as we know them today grew out of the scandal-mongering sheets of the eighteenth century and quite probably the broadsheets of an earlier time. Their origins were much nearer the grassroots than in the case of the book. The issue of the first daily newspaper was the *Daily courant* which was issued on the 11th March, 1702.

The eighteenth century also saw the development of the periodical of which the most notable were Sir Richard Steele's *The tatler* (1709); Joseph Addison's *Spectator* (1711) and Roderick Cave's *Gentleman's magazine* (1731). These periodicals were aimed at the rising commercial middle class. They were alo remarkable for the fact that they gave an impetus to the English essay as a literary genre. The essays were light, witty and discursive, treating of topics in a meditative and highly personalised fashion and many of the essays were intended for women readers. Cynthia White (11) is quite firm on the point that Steele's *Tatler* was the ancestor of the magazine for women readers. Later periodicals were to be less flippant in their content and intentions: John Wilke's *North Briton* (1762) was to sow the seeds of a radical journalism which was to be an important force in the nineteenth century politics, exemplified in William Cobbett's *Political register* (1802). Both periodicals raised the point of freedom of expression; both men were jailed for the publication of their newspapers.

This historical fact introduces a new and important concept into our discussion: both newspapers and periodicals depended upon technical innovation, but they also depended upon liberty. This factor was particularly crucial in a period of industrial and political turmoil when the British government, fearful of the political doctrines of the French Revolution, used both financial and political oppression to silence any newspaper or periodical which seemed to be hostile, or even critical of, the established social and political order. In 1785 was founded one of the most remarkable journalistic institutions in history. *The times*, which was first published under the title of the *Daily universal register*, was conceived by its founder, John Walter, as a newsheet concerning itself with scandal and commercial intelligence. His son John Walter II had very different ideas. With its famed editor, Thomas Barnes, he built *The times* into an information medium geared to the tastes and values of the rising middle classes. Barnes was probably the first journalist to recognise the power of public opinion when properly channelled through a newspaper, and made 'the Thunderer' a powerful voice in the struggle for reform.

By the time he was succeeded by J T Delane it was the government who feared *The times* rather than the reverse. This newspaper was to show for the first time the importance of the linkage between information and political decisions, which is a significant feature of a democratic state. William Howard Russell's stirring reports on the mismanagement of the Crimean war brought down the cabinet of 1855, and destroyed the political career of Lord Aberdeen.

The growth of political consciousness gave a strong psychological incentive to the growth of mass literacy. Altick (12) tells us that every miner carried a copy of the *Black dwarf*, a radical underground newspaper founded by Wooller. The underground press is by no means a twentieth century phenomenon. By the early 1840's a distinctive Sunday press had emerged to catch up and continue the content of the popular chapbooks and ballads. The removal of the crippling stamp tax in 1855 not only assisted the *Daily telegraph* on its career, but timed in nicely with the development of more sophisticated techniques in the printing industry and the spread of the railways to provide more rapid distribution facilities. This latter mention of speed leads to the discussion of another medium of communication which was to have a profound influence on the formation of a mass society.

7.6 PHYSICAL COMMUNICATION SYSTEMS

In dealing with the growth spiral which characterises the mass media, the importance of physical communications systems can never be over-emphasised. The Roman empire was held together by its postal service, the *cursus publicus*; and in medieval times the universities ran their own postal services. It was, however, a service exclusive to an elite; the majority were illiterate and did not have the ability to communicate with one another by the written word. It was not until the seventeenth century that the broader social needs were emphasised and, in 1633, a regular mail service was set up between London, Antwerp and Brussels which took from four to five days. It was such a service that enabled the members of the Royal Society and other like-minded institutions to correspond with one another. The improvement in roads and physical communications at the end of the eighteenth century helped the growth of such new papers as *The times* and *The observer*, by facilitating accessibility to a greater range of distribution.

Physical communications are in themselves forms of mass communication. People can travel and they can learn more about other people; conversely, railways can also help to destroy regional communities and cultures. The spread of railway travel in Britain can be linked with the growth of two great commercial circulating libraries—Mudies (1852) and W H Smith (1843). Their importance, which increased as the century went on, had two signal characteristics: they helped to increase the reading habit and their monopolistic role gave them considerable power of veto over what could be published. Their orders could often determine a publisher's decision whether to publish a book or not. The power of governments over the printed word was beginning to devolve upon the large commercial organisations. Railways did not only convey printed materials to distribution centres, they also used and helped to develop the telegraph. With telegraph, newspapers large and small, city and provincial became closer to equal access to sources of information. Gradually it liberated provincial printers from being the passive consumers of weeks-old information from the larger cities. Both in the mechanics of printing and in physical communications, the operative word became *speed*.

In 1837, Morse demonstrated his new system of telegraphy, and within a few years telegraph lines linked the major American cities, helping to bring the new country into a coherent administrative unit. In 1866 Europe and America were linked for the first time. This invention not only generated speed in transmitting messages across space, but equally worthy of note was the speed with which the invention was adopted. The staple of contemporary economic values was the use of technical innovation in the interest of capital

154

accumulation and, correspondingly, there was an increase in capital investment. The accompanying sociological feature was the formation of large companies to develop each innovation.

In 1851, the year of the Great Exhibition, the stock exchanges of London and Paris were connected by telegraph so that prices could be rapidly compared. This fact illustrates a vital point about the speed of information transfer and the nineteenth century grasp of commercial possibilities. In a competitive society, speed was of primary value; not only could it aid effective decision making, but also it could quell rumour in a field of activity where rumour could be disastrous. The war of 1812 between Great Britain and America was caused by the lack of such a facility (13), and it is this thought that may well have been influential in the setting up of the teletype hotline between Washington and Moscow.

What is interesting for the student is the examination of the interrelationships between new and old media. The introduction of a new medium never entirely supplants another; it may even enhance the efficiency of the older one. In the same year as that of the Great Exhibition, Paul Julius Reuter organized his commercial wire service, resulting in the formation of that most fascinating of information centres, the news agency.

The three modes of communication which were to characterize the industrial society in the nineteenth century were the railway, the telegraph and more latterly, the telephone. Distance was becoming increasingly irrelevant in the administration of large political units. The British empire most certainly had communicative advantages over its illustrious predecessor the Roman empire. Colin Cherry (14) puts this point: 'At one stroke the speed of messages were raised by some ten million times by the telegraph, from that of the horse to that of electricity.'

The history of the newspaper provides a useful teaching illustration of how the invention of a new medium can increase the efficiency of an older one. The development of the photographic process which originated in the pioneering work of Niepce and Daguerre led to its success as a mass circulation tabloid in the latter decade of the nineteenth century. Print could now be supported by the visual illustration, both in the learned journal and in comic strip for the semi-literate, a device which Northcliffe used for the first time in the *Daily mirror* in 1904.

Technically speaking the telephone is an extension of the

telegraph. Indeed, the first microphone, made by the German, Philip Reiss, operated rather in the manner of a high-speed telegraph; the sound-waves of the voice 'making' and 'breaking' an electric current—a device popularly called the 'bang bang principle'. Credit is usually given to Alexander Graham Bell for the invention of what we now know as the telephone. The circumstances of this invention provide for the student a classic case study in the sociology of research and development. It was not plucked out of a social vacuum; the scientific principles on which it was founded were known for decades before 1876. The historic and the economic milieu were so much on the inventor's side that they nearly overwhelmed him. He had the stimulus of fierce competition from other men who saw, or thought they saw, how to capitalise on existing scientific knowledge to develop the telephone. But none of them enjoyed Bell's unique combination of qualities: so perfect claims Robert Bruce (15) in his classic study, that if some super-computer had been able to select the telephone's most likely inventor, it would have chosen Bell. He lived in a community of enterprising capitalists; he possessed unusual drive and energy, a keen hearing, and a sense of pitch. He was a trained pianist with a deep knowledge of telegraphy. Most of all, he lived in a society eager for rapid communication. What also emerges from Bruce's classic study is Bell's absorbing interest in the communication problems of the deaf.

The telephone and the telegraph had two things in common: both used wires; and both were essentially interpersonal communication systems. At the close of the nineteenth century the newspaper, the magazine and the book were still the chief media of communication. The next logical step was the introduction of wireless telegraphy, which led eventually to the medium we know today as radio. In 1901 Guglielmo Marconi succeeded in establishing a wireless link between America and Europe; in 1903 Lee de Forest invented the triode thermionic valve; and with the impetus provided by the First World War the concept of the wireless as a means of entertainment and communication was born.

In the strict sense of the term, radio was the first mass communication medium; that is, in reaching the maximum audience in the minimum time. It is doubtful if the book was ever a 'mass' medium in this way. The development of radio brought an old term back in to current usage: the term was 'broadcast'. The sower in the parable cast the seed abroad instead of sowing it in drills. It is this 'spraying' element which informs the modern restrictive definition of mass media of communication. One man can monopolise a book, or a newspaper, he cannot monopolise a radio broadcast. Indeed, if he lives in China, he may find it hard to avoid the information which is being transmitted to all and sundry. In much the same way that wire communications gave rise to wireless, radio gave rise to an interest in television, where it coalesced with another medium. In 1895 the Lumiere brothers developed the cinematograph and their technical discovery was complemented by the creative imagination of George Melies. It was left to John Baird to transfer the idea of the institutional to the domestic in the form of the television.

If one looks at the rapid development of communications in the western world, it is difficult to avoid using the term 'explosion'. Johann Gutenberg was printing with movable types by the middle of the fifteenth century, but more than three and a half centuries were to elapse before there was any change in the fundamental design of his press. *The times* added the power of steam to the process; thereby facilitating the mass production of printed materials. The next seventy years saw continents linked by sophisticated communications systems.

Organised broadcasting began in the 1920's in both Great Britain and America, and the first regular television service was started by the BBC in 1936. Within thirty years of this date 'Early Bird' was in orbit and had been used to transmit television pictures across the Atlantic. Three years later men were receiving television pictures from the moon. The functional advantages of the satellite were too obvious to be ignored: they are much better than cables for transmitting microwaves. The trouble with microwaves is that they travel in straight lines; they cannot bend round buildings or follow the curvature of the earth. They must therefore be shunted from one relay tower to another. A satellite in line of sight of a third of the globe is an ideal microwave station, it needs less power than a terrestrial tower and the signals travel in a straight line from it.

It is small wonder that McLuhan in his enthusiasm pictured the world as 'a global village'. There was a time when satellites were science fiction until the idea was put forward in a feasible form by Arthur C Clarke (16) in 1945. The computer, which has been in the popular mythology since the early 1950's, was soon to move into the world of communications. As Maddox (17) remarks, 'it moved into

157

the communications industry by the back door'. The newest telephone exchanges are nothing less than computers in themselves. Computer typesetting is fast becoming the norm, and the information problems of the newsagency were ripe for its ministrations.

The one point which this breathless gallop may serve to illustrate to the student is the extreme rapidity of change in communications technology. This change is not something remote from his professional practice as a librarian. Each of the inventions outlined in the fore-going has produced some new material with the attendant problems of storage and retrieval. This point can be used to show the diversity of ways in which information has been recorded and help to remove the stereotyped connotation of a library as containing nothing else but books.

At this juncture in the discussion it may be helpful to draw an analogy between the mass media systems and public library systems. The development of the mass media was roughly co-eval with the development of the public library concept in Great Britain. Both systems benefited from the newly-literate audiences created by the development of mass literacy in the nineteenth century. Both systems provide an equality of access to social information which, in pre-industrial societies, was filtered down through the social hierarchy. Both systems need to study their audience's needs; both assume an advanced degree of literacy and technical expertise in their planning and operations, which makes their transplanting to an underdeveloped region an extremely difficult enterprise.

The mass media constitute a major part of the environment in which librarianship is practised. For Denis McQuail (18) they are: 'The entire systems within which messages are produced, selected, transmitted and responded to'. This term can be used in the widest sense to denote public television, radio, the large circulation press, the cinema and gramophone records. A more restrictive definition denotes radio and television as those media which reach the maximum number of people in the shortest time. The idea of the 'mass' is that their content reaches all sorts and conditions of men, as distinct from a communication intended for a certain elite or set of interests either social or intellectual. The media developed over little more than a century, as we have seen, starting with the mass circulation press. Each medium had a rising curve of diffusion and each new one spread more rapidly than its predecessor. Television ownership both in Britain and the United States grew to near saturation point in the period 1948 to 1960 and television has now become the dominant mass medium in almost all advanced industrial countries. It also provided an example of a medium of communication imposing a certain pattern of social behaviour on its users. Belson, using the evidence obtained by the BBC Audience Research Department showed that by 1959, viewing in Britain had reached an average daily level of two and a half hours per person (19).

The experience of countries undergoing development is a highly relevant point for discussion in this module, as it acquaints the student with the problems of international and comparative librarianship; a subject in which he may wish to specialize at a later stage of the course. Like libraries, the mass media are of importance to the new country aspiring to sophisticated industrialisation; except that the mass media may have an advantage over the library in assuming a lesser degree of literacy. The spread of the mass media is highly correlated with several indices of development: literacy rates, urbanisation, *per capita* income and industrialisation. Instead of working in opposing directions they can become allies in the diffusion of information relevant to social change. Those students interested in the plight of the third world should be interested to note that the mass media, like sophisticated library services, tend to be exclusive to those nations constituting the 'rich man's club'; that is, variations between countries in levels of economic developments are closely paralleled by variations in the levels of media availability.

According to Wilbur Schramm (20), a comparison of the world's three most underdeveloped regions (Africa, Asia and South America) with the four most developed (USA, Japan, Western Europe, Australia) showed the latter to have per hundred persons, 600% more newspapers; 970% more radio sets; 690% more cinema seats and eighteen times more television sets. The lesson to be drawn is a salutary one for the student who has any convictions at all regarding the social role of his profession in the dissemination of information. One can see, in surveying the historical development of the media, how each new communications technology has influenced library practice and problems. Such a model, though simplistic, and perhaps a little contrived, should provide a stimulus for further thought and serve to bring together the materials in the previous

MEDIUM	LIBRARY MATERIALS	LIBRARY PROBLEM
Artifacts	Realia	Storage and cataloguing problems.
Writing (scribing)	Manuscripts	Specialised bibliographic and cataloguing procedures.
Printing	Books, journals	Importance of authorship in retrieval strategy. Utilization of sources of information. The title page as the standard in cataloguing.
Railways	Timetables	Influence on townplanning; access to libraries and materials. Mobility of staff.
Telephone	Directories	Influence on reference library information procedures, and on library administration.
Photography	Photographs; micro-films; filmstrips	Storage and retrieval problems.
Phonograph (Gramophone)	Gramophone records	Music librarianship; specialised cataloguing rules. Influence on library education.
Cinema	Films	Special forms of librarianship. The resource centre concept. Ancillary to book in teaching and information transfer.
Radio	Audio tapes	Use in providing services for the blind.
Television	Video Cassettes	Shares with films and cassettes the problems of storage and analytical indexing.
Computers	Computer tapes, discs etc.	Computerised storage and retrieval: linguistic problems. The influence of the computer on library management procedures.

THE HISTORICAL DEVELOPMENT OF THE MEDIA WITH
REFERENCE TO LIBRARY PROBLEMS

chapters.

The lefthand column shows the historical development of the media; the centre column the product and the third the attendant problems of organization storage and retrieval.

Although man has stored his thoughts in symbolic form since the first stage of communications explosion, it was not until the nineteenth century that there was any method of storing the human voice or the events of history as seen by the camera. These two communications functions could be used to organise, in a meaningful framework, what otherwise might be a dreary list of dates.

The eye and human movement

1822 Nicephore Niepce makes the first photograph. Seven years later he begins work with Jacques Daguerre.

1839 Journals appear with photographs.

1841 Fox Talbot patents the calotype or positive negative process for photography.

1871 Siege of Paris. Microfilm first used to send messages by beleaguered defenders.

1884 George Eastman invents the roll film.

1895 The Lumiere brothers invent the first practical motion picture systems.

1915 D W Griffiths' film *Birth of a nation* develops new cinematographic techniques.

1923 Vladimir Zworykin invents the ionoscope and the kinescope; the one for transmitting, the other for receiving messages.

1923 John Baird transmits silhouettes by television.

1927 Warner brothers produce first talkie starring Al Jolson, thereby uniting sound and vision.

The voice: storage and transmission

1876 Alexander Graham Bell invents the telephone.

1878 Thomas Edison invents the cylindrical phonograph.

1889 Edward Branly invents the coherer, furthering the practical development of wireless communications.

1901 Marconi sends wireless signals across the Atlantic.

1903 Arthur Korn transmits images by telegraph.

1920 First broadcasts by Marconi Company from Chelmsford, Essex.

1922 British Broadcasting Company founded. Lord Reith appointed managing director.

161

1923 *Radio times* started.

1927 British Broadcasting Corporation founded.

1929 *The listener* started by J C W Reith to preserve and disseminate the more valuable broadcast material.

1936 First transmission of regular television programmes from Alexandra Palace, London.

1954 British commercial television started.

Communication through time

1582 Pope Gregory XIII introduces the Gregorian calendar.

1799 Discovery of the Rosetta Stone, key to the decipherment of Egyptian hieroglyphics.

1822 The French scholar Jean Champollion, using the rosetta stone, deciphers Egyptian hieroglyphics.

1846 Sir Henry Rawlinson publishes his work on the cuneiform inscription of the Behistun rock, found in Persia.

1952 Michael Ventris and John Chadwick decipher Linear B the Creto-Mycenaean script.

1960 Russian astronomers use computers in their effort to decipher Mayan writing.

1 W Kornhauser *The politics of mass society* New York, Free Press,1959.

2 Emile Durkheim *The division of labour in society* translated by G. Simpson, New York, MacMillan, 1933.

3 F Tonnies *Community and association* London, Routledge, 1955.

4 David Landes *The unbound Proeetheus: technological and industrial change in western Europe from 1750 to the present* Cambridge, Cambridge University Press, 1969.

5 John U Nef *War and human progress* New York, Norton, 1968.

6 Lewis Mumford *Technics and civilization* New York, Harcourt, Brace, 1963.

7 E P Thompson 'Time work – discipline and industrial capitalism' in *Past and present* 38, Dec 1967, p 57-97.

8 David Landes *Op cit*

9 Arthur Koestler *The act of creation* London, Hutchinson, 1964.

10 J Daniels 'The big questions in the historiography of American technology' *Technology and culture* 11 (1) January 1970, p 4.

11 Cynthia L White *Women's magazines 1693-1968* London, Michael Joseph, 1970.

12 Richard Altick *The English common reader* Chicago University Press, 1962.

13 T A Bailey *Diplomatic history of the American people* New York, Meredith, 1964.

14 Colin Cherry *World communications* New York, Wiley, 1970, p 48.

15 Robert Bruce *Alexander Graham Bell and the conquest of solitude* London, Gollancz, 1973.

16 In *Wireless world* October 1945.

17 Brenda Maddox *Communications: the next revolution* London, The economist,1970.

18 Denis McQuail *Towards a sociology of mass communications* London, MacMillan, 1969, p 4.

19 W A Belson *The impact of television* London, Crosby Lockwood, 1968.
20 W Schramm *Mass media and national development* Stanford, Stanford University Press, 1964.

CHAPTER 8

Mass communications
and social information systems

THIS OUR last chapter, is put forward as an attempted synthesis of
the concepts discussed in the previous chapters and is centred round
two main questions:

How do the mass media function as information systems?

What is the relevance of mass media research for the librarian?

One of the most significant characteristics of the transition from
pre-industrial community to industrial society was the change in the
modes of communication. As we have noted in chapter seven, in the
rigidly structured world of the community, information was
gradually *filtered* down through the social hierarchy. In modern
society, mass communications *diffuse* information from a central
point in the social structure to all its members; and this information,
like the rain, falls on the just and the unjust alike. But the primitive
tribe had a watcher on the hillside to warn its members of imminent
danger. The fireside had acted as a forum for the discussion of tribal
problems and also served as an informal school for the young who
gathered to listen to their elders. Both social systems possess
communications elites, in the case of the tribe it was the elders or
'priesthood'; in industrial society, the elite is composed of
professional communicators. These professional communicators
decide what is to be communicated, and the way in which it should
be presented.

The social phenomenon of the mass communications system has
now become a study engaging the interests of specialists from many
disciplines. The psychologist, who investigates the effects of the
media; the literary critic, who scrutinizes the moral and aesthetic
standards of the media content; and the sociologist, who attempts to
obtain a synoptic view of the interplay between a society and its
system of mass communications. Mass communication theory is also
an area of interest to the librarian, since both mass communicator

164

and librarian are engaged in communication activities and, as an aid to this investigation, we use the wider framework of the sociologist.

8.2 FUNCTIONAL ANALYSIS AND THE MEDIA

The principal approach adopted by the sociologist is to analyse the functions of the mass media in society. He examines questions of media control and the consequences of this organisation for society. He asks such questions as: 'How are people's relationships influenced by the mass media?' 'How does the mass media system fit into the social process?' Functional analysis has two meanings in sociology. Its major use can be seen in the following statement: 'The social function of religion is the maintenance of group solidarity'. Here it is asserted that a social phenomenon such as religion has a demonstrable part to play in holding society together. The other use of the term function is somewhat analogous to the mathematical use of the term eg X is a function of Y. When social phenomenon X is a function of social phenomenon Y it means that X varies in proportion as Y does.

Functionalism views a social institution as a component of a larger system. A sociological analysis of the library in society might usefully adopt a functional approach, asking what effect the library has on social control; or what kind of a society might be assumed should the library not exist either in concept or in actuality. The antecedents of functionalism in sociology are well illustrated by the saying of Voltaire that 'if there were no God, man would have had to invent him'. The first substantial proposal for a funtional analysis of mass communications was given by Lasswell (1) in which he distinguishes three main functions:

1 The surveillance of the environment.
2 The correlation of society in responding to the environment.
3 The transmission of the social heritage from one generation to the next.

Lasswell sees the functions of social communication as surveillance, consensus and socialization. However, the two main agents are the sender and the receiver and it might be useful to group the intentions of both parties under headings such as these:

FROM THE SENDER'S VIEWPOINT	FROM THE RECEIVER'S VIEWPOINT
Objectives	Objectives
1 To inform	1 To understand
2 To teach	2 To learn

165

3 To please	3 To enjoy
4 To persuade	4 To weigh and consider before making a decision.

These communication activities have certain results for the cultural repertoire of society and for the individual's contribution.

RESULTS FOR SOCIETY	RESULTS FOR THE INDIVIDUAL
1 Enables society to share a common knowledge of the environment.	1 Enriches the personality.
2 Helps to induct new members of society into social roles and skills.	2 Helps the individual acquire skills and knowledge.
3 Entertains members of society; serves as a safety valve for social pressures and creates artistic form.	3 Enjoyment and relaxation creative use of leisure.
4 Helps society gain a working consensus on social and political decisions especially in the case of social innovation or times of crisis.	4 Presents the individual with sufficient information for democratic decision-making.

These functions are performed in varying degrees of intensity by the library when it is fulfilling its social role, and a comparative analysis of the functions of public libraries and mass media serves as a helpful basis for seminar discussions. The function of the mass media has not radically altered since primitive tribal times. Lasswell's three functions can be summarised as the newsgathering activities, the weather forecasts and other information which enables a society to be alert to environmental problems and plan accordingly. The mass media can also be used to establish a social consensus and thereby act as an agency of social control; for example, in time of war.

8.3 MASS MEDIA: CHARACTERISTICS

A useful exercise at this stage would be to analyse the characteristics of the media and attempt to locate analogies with a large public library service. The media serve a wide and heterogenous audience with all the attendant problems of selecting suitable material for every level of interest and educational ability. In order to overcome this disadvantage the communication content is centred upon some imaginary reference point in order to achieve some common denominator.

This policy is much in line with the cynical New York editor who told his staff to 'write for the guy who moves his lips when he reads'. In terms of communication theory the more widely diverse the audience the greater the difficulty in forming an image coherent enough to assist the communicator in selecting the appropriate content. The problems of the public librarian and his specialist colleague can be usefully compared within this framework. The public librarian serves a heterogeneous audience and, like the mass communicator, he is beset by problems of scope and level in his selection of material. The special library librarian is, at the very least, serving a clientele with common objectives.

Because the mass media are capable of reaching vast and widespread audiences, there is a need for fewer individual media. To transmit a message by word of mount through the whole of Great Britain would take a great deal of time and involve a great many chains of human interaction; a single broadcasting network can do the same job in seconds. This problem, as Peterson (2) points out, has its parallel in the industrial sphere where relatively few manufacturers can turn out astronomically large numbers of standardised products. The concentration of communication centres is now becoming a feature of library organisation both in the public and special fields, resulting in fewer centres for the diffusion of information. This phenomenon is largely the result of the development of physical communication systems.

Time was when county libraries were regarded as the Cinderella of library services with a motley clientele of horsey county ladies and rustics. As physical communications systems changed, so also did county library structures and the social composition of their users. As Berryman (3) points out this also gave many county library systems the opportunity of re-thinking their social roles. The mass communicator suffers from the disadvantage of lack of contact with his audience and has set about remedying this deficiency; the librarian has let years of opportunity slip by in not getting to know his audience and in omitting to make user studies an integral part of professional education and training.

The mass media are organized to allow communication to flow in one direction or as Larsen (4) puts it: 'the ratio of output to input is very large'. It is therefore necessary for the mass communicator to devise certain mechanisms for reducing this uncertainty in the communicator—audience relationship. The result has been the impressive panoply associated with audience analysis questionnaires and in-depth interviews; techniques which are now part of the *modus operandi* of the special librarian. The public library, because of its very nature, suffers from the greatest degree of uncertainty regarding the social composition and information needs of its users. Writers of library textbooks have been content to expatiate at length on the behaviour of a convenient abstraction called 'the general reader' who obligingly consults indexes and returns borrowed material on time. There are signs that this passive attitude towards the audience is changing both in special and in public libraries.

An instance of this approach is the classic work by Lowell Martin (5) in Chicago. The object of his survey was to identify user groups within the community and analyse their respective needs. The underlying policy in his report is that Chicago Public Library should retain its multipurpose philosophy, but add the necessary specialities to carry and intensify service to the various identifiable segments within the population. In other words, Chicago Public Library would become a network of special libraries, adapted to these distinct groups and interests that characterized such a wide and diverse population. In Great Britain, Brian Luckham has been attempting research in the same area and at the London and Home Counties Branch management course at Woburn in 1970, the idea of a Public Libraries Research Group was started (6). The intention was to restate some of the traditional public library objectives to which not only a management framework could be applied, but from which valid systems of output measurement could logically emerge. The group now acts as a steering committee for the Hillingdon Project (7). This research project originally started off as a research scheme to be conducted into the areas of co-operation and integration which could exist between public and academic libraries, and later evolved into a much wider concept. Basically it is a research study on user satisfaction, achieved by measuring the effectiveness of all types of library service within a given community and developing a valid methodology for the attainment of this end. Reasons for the use and non-use of libraries have been considered, with samples in depth taken from different types of user. In the special library field, user studies are now an industry in themselves, with a growing corpus of literature. It can be seen then that the

168

discussion of media-audience relationships has a demonstrable teaching value in allowing a teacher and student to transfer the problem from the field of mass communications to those of library services.

The demand by the mass media for a high level of research activity in audience measurement can readily be appreciated. Although the press and the cinema can operate without audience research, basing their operations on evidence of sales and attendance, in practice some research is inevitable if the market is to be fully exploited, especially in highly competitive conditions. The link between the newspaper, the periodical press and advertising has led to much research into the social composition of audience groups. Newspapers can only operate if they have continuous and detailed information about the location interests and income levels of their readers (8). It should require little proof that these social data are necessary for the planning and organization of a socially aware public library service. The requirements of broadcasting are even more stringent, since without later research there is no proof of the existence of an audience, let alone its lifestyle and social composition.

One of the most common and universal themes in social criticism today is the association of the mass media with unwelcome societal tendencies. The media are accused of manipulation, and of purveying content which is responsible for aggression, alienation and a host of crimes. Beneath these accusations lies the assumption that the media are *active* agents acting upon a *passive* audience; an assumption which a course might profitably explore. Criticism of the mass media between the two world wars tended to see the media as shooting 'magic bullets' into the powerless minds of the audience, but the research of postwar psychologists led to the idea that the individual is not as easily influenced or manipulated as had been commonly supposed. Very often the media do little else but reinforce existing attitudes.

This area of research is of particular relevance to the public librarian who is almost invariably involved in the problem of censoring materials that may have a tendency to deprave and corrupt. Two of the early researchers in this field were Elihu Katz and Paul Lazarsfeld (9) whose ideas were first triggered off by a study of persuasive techniques used in the American Presidential campaign of 1940. Elections in a democratic state are a classic case of information used as persuasion, and of the use of selected information in argument with the purpose of changing attitudes. The researches of Katz and Lazarsfeld led them to formulate the hypothesis that people exposed themselves only to information that fitted in with their preconceptions and attitudes; if they did not agree with the information presented they simply ignored it.

The lesson for the student of the sociology of information is that efficient channels are not sufficient in themselves. The human concept system is far more complex and intractable than the early mass communicators and propagandists had ever anticipated. The points discussed in Chapter two are very relevant here and it may sound trite to mention again that man is pre-eminently a social animal and that this applies to his reception of information. We are often misled by the notion that the term 'information' implies some pure ethereal entity far removed from the sordidness of the human condition. In journals dealing with librarianship, it is frequently cited in a scientific context which again gives the impression that it relates exclusively to abstruse mathematical formulae or to proven facts which are beyond dispute.

Like the electronic media, information is ethically neutral until the human concept system puts it to use. The same applies to propaganda or any other technique which uses information as persuasion. Information can be used to persuade people that the influx of emigrants will mean a decline in their standards of living; information can also be used to persuade people to join a literacy compaign, or a scheme to raise the standards of personal hygiene. Even the smallest branch library has some books where someone is trying to persuade somebody else to think or act in certain ways.

The findings regarding the way people receive information, which Katz and Lazarsfeld initiated, culminated in the now famous 'two step flow' or 'n-step flow of information'. In every community there are some people who are more influential than others, who have travelled more or who are more knowledgeable; these people the sociologists call 'influentials' or 'opinion leaders'. These people need not necessarily have an ascribed superior position or rank in a hierarchy, very often they are just rank and file members. This concept of the function of individuals in information flow became of increasing importance, not only in mass communications studies, but also in management theory and in organizations which set out to initiate innovation whether in suburbia or in the remote regions of some underdeveloped country.

There is now a growing literature of case studies in innovation procedures, and professional communicators have found that people's attitudes are not changed simply by showering them with leaflets or blaring new ideas at them from a radio van. Many a chief librarian has found that if he wishes to initiate a drastic change or innovation, memos and notices are not enough; nor is it always sufficient to obtain the assent of his immediate subordinates. There is also a hidden hierarchy of opinion among the juniors which every efficient manager should be aware of. To induce reluctant peasants to change their agricultural methods is an exercise in the communication of information. The source has the necessary information, but he also wishes it to be understood, accepted and acted upon. Bearing in mind the capacity of the individual for imitation, he may decide to transmit the information to selected individuals who are deemed to have status in the community and use them as the first step in the 'flow'.

The strongest development of the selective exposure hypothesis was made by Leon Festinger (10) in his 'theory of cognitive dissonance'. According to this theory, every individual has a 'cognitive map' which is a quintessence of his emotional and intellectual upbringing, social beliefs and personal experience. He does not therefore receive information in its pristine state, but always through a filter system. While this cognitive map is orderly and symmetrical the individual is in a state of 'consonance'; that is, he is at peace with the world. When he is exposed to information which forces him to redraw this map he is said to be in a state of 'dissonance' and can resolve this intellectual discomfort either by rejecting the flow of information or by selecting certain items that fit into his cognitive map.

I doubt if this theory accounts for all the relationships between information and attitude change, but it does show the importance of information theory in psychology, and particularly in the psychology of information transmission. One wonders, therefore, if the term 'information transfer' can be validly and accurately used with reference to the communication between two human beings. Whether one takes Festinger's theory at its face value or not, every individual has a screening device which enables him to process distasteful messages and make them acceptable to his view of the world.

One of the significant features of twentieth century industrial

171

society is the function of the mass media as message bearing systems, and the power of the media to regulate the flow of information within society. If one uses an organic analogy of the workings of society, the media could be compared with the human sensory system. When a state wishes to change its monetary system, initiate a new pensions scheme, or organise any innovation, it uses the media as communication channels—working on the assumption that its members will have access to these media. The British system can be used as a teaching model to identify the merits and defects of the major media in transferring information from the rulers to those who are ruled; and, in a democratic state, making sure that there is an *upward* flow of information as well. The enquiry can centre on three main areas:

1 The interrelationships between the major media: television, radio and newspapers.
2 The problems of the media as channels of information.
3 The interdependence of mass communication and personal communication systems.

Unlike its elder brother the newspaper, radio was born into a comparatively democratic society; it had no Star Chamber and no crippling Stamp Tax to stunt its growth. Like so many new inventions it was welcomed as a toy by the newspaper barons such as Northcliffe and Beaverbrook. Suddenly the idea dawned on them that radio could transmit news at a speed far greater than that of the newspaper, and the result was pressure on the government to prevent the BBC from giving its news bulletins until late in the evening when the last editions of the newspapers were off the streets.

The new medium of the radio needed a personality to give it a philosophy and a sense of direction and it found such a man in J C W Reith. For this 'son of the manse' the medium had a threefold purpose: education, information and entertainment; a similar philosophy could be attributed to public libraries. Reith conceived radio as an instrument of social betterment, as a means of enlarging the range of public information, of elevating public taste and safeguarding public morality. In order to achieve these aims he stressed that radio must be a public service and monopoly; a communicating institution that could select its material without worrying about the size of its audience and which could operate safely beyond the arbitrary whim of the advertiser. However controversial this paternalistic philosophy may have been, it

172

considerably influenced the ethos of public service broadcasting in Great Britain.

The concept of a public information system is directly linked to the concept of participatory democracy; indeed information and democracy are interdependent ideas. The government of a modern industrial state involves the handling of enormous quantities of information, in which the librarians in government libraries play their part. A further dimension enters the course at this stage. The way information is handled is very often a political matter which brings our brief discussion into the murky waters of political theory. If one may dare to coin a new phrase, here is an area which for want of a better term could be called the 'ethics of information', which evolves about such questions as:

How much information should an organization release?

To what steps should a government go to ensure that every citizen fully understands his or her rights?

To what degree should the media edit the information they receive?

What criteria should be used in selecting and presenting information on controversial topics?

Topics such as these foregoing provide a useful framework of analysis for the student and their importance for the librarian needs little demonstration. There is a considerable bibliography on the problems of the censorship of erotic and pornographic materials, and even a cursory glance at the professional literature of librarianship shows an abiding interest in this problem. What is so often neglected is the problem of the *censorship of information* whether actively, in order to suit some political purpose, or by default when the failure to provide adequate information channels deprives some citizens of their rights. The British national health service is an admirable institution, founded on a philosophy of compassion for the weaker members of the human race, but as Brian Abel Smith (11) has shown, the people who benefit mostly from its ministrations are the people who know where to obtain the maximum amount of information; these people are usually the middle classes for whom it was not primarily intended.

As society becomes more complex, so it necessarily needs more information channels to function efficiently. It also necessarily generates more information. There would seem to be an opening here for a kind of 'librarianship outside the walls', the librarian acting as an 'information broker' or 'social information officer', carrying to a logical conclusion the function which, voluntary and official advice centres and public reference libraries have fulfilled in the past. To do this, the traditional concept of the reference library must be extended to that of the 'community information centre'. But to be well informed requires time and leisure; indeed, for the ordinary man to be a fully competent political agent he would need to make a profession of being well informed.

It is assumed that a firmly established parliamentary democracy rests on the active participation of a substantial number of men and women and entails the capacity for informed acts of choice. This kind of decision making can only take place where people are made aware of the full range of choices available and have access to all relevant information. There are two dangers here of which every librarian should be aware. As the amount of information increases even the most energetic intellect may be tempted to withdraw completely with the excuse that it is all too much. Social psychologists call this withdrawal syndrome, 'privatisation', meaning a passive acceptance of decision making made by others on the individual's behalf, because the situation has become too complex. There is a favourite theme of Marshall McLuhan's that children in contemporary society are deprived in the paradoxical sense that they suffer from 'information overload' and school provides no remedy for this. In contrast with preceding centuries the level of knowledge outside the classroom is higher than that inside. The other danger is that the decision makers may become increasingly remote from the people on whose behalf they make the decisions and may be snared by the delusion that an efficient communications technology is a panacea for all information problems.

These considerations provide a new dimension for the librarian in a society which, in McLuhan's terms, is suffering from 'information overload'. Though administrative agencies of business and government are becoming ever more remote to the individual in society, the ability of these bodies to pinpoint and examine each member of a community as a specimen on a slide increases with the aid of computerised information stores. In other words 'they know about you even if you don't know about them' and, as Malcolm Warner (12) points out, the social scientist and the computer scientist have combined to produce a background to action on the

174

part of the individual citizen as well as the social administrator, the political decision maker, and the information technologist.

Integrated data banks covering the life details of whole populations are now a technical and social feasibility. If the Department of Health wishes to computerise data on every patient using the health service, it may legitimately claim that the survey data are for planning; on the other hand, it does not need much imagination to foresee the manipulative facility in the hands of a less benevolent government. As Warner states, information handling on a computerised basis is a 'low visibility operation'; an individual may never discover that he is the subject of a file or be given any precise knowledge of what is in it.

A free and critical mass media could be a safeguard against this assault on privacy. Yet the media are seen by many democratic governments as a menace to the autonomy of their legislative assemblies, not as a means for the assemblies to get in touch with the people and counter the malaise of apathy, which is said to afflict the people of many countries. The media in themselves are accused of deceit: they are credited with having a 'narcotizing dysfunction'. That is, they create an illusion of participation and contact with reality, through an oversupply of trivia masquerading as important information. By providing a substitute for action, they act as a social narcotic and as an agency of social illusion.

8.4 NEWS SELECTION AND THE MEDIA

The question which arises at this stage is, 'how does the information reach the media, and how is it selected?' The media, whether it be newspaper, radio, or television must select from the uncountable number of events which are happening in the world at any particular time. Like the human information system they cannot take in everything, and the wider their audience the greater the difficulty. The editor of the home town community newspaper has a frame of reference to guide him in his selection procedures. There is an analogy here with the problem of the librarian as selector of materials. He cannot take in every publication and so must contrive to form a basis for selection. This brings us into an area called the 'sociology of organizations' which students will encounter in library management courses.

The core concept, on which most of the published work is based, is that of the 'gatekeeper'. This term, which has been borrowed by many other subjects, was coined by Kurt Lewin (13), the famous social psychologist. Lewin's initial studies in the flow of communication within organizations led him on to the study of news and the mass media. Information must flow through certain channels, and at certain places within these channels there are 'gates' through which news might or might not be admitted. The editor of a newspaper or journal is a gatekeeper, so also is the producer of our nightly news bulletins.

Communication organisations are not inanimate entities, they are composed of people interacting with other people; and within these organisations are elite groups and opinion leaders, just as in any community. The 'gatekeeper' in a news organisation is confronted with a wide variety of choices and a wide array of items for inclusion. He may be influenced by the following:

His own personal values and background

His image of the requirements of his audience

The sanctions and pressures of his organisation

His role in the organisation

The librarian as selector of materials may be influenced by the same constraints, and this parallel has too much teaching value to be ignored. Both communicator and librarian must have images of their respective audiences; both are subject to social and economic restraints. Both are faced with varying levels of ability and diversity of interests within their audience. Where the parallel ends, however, is in the area of audience research. There the professional communicators have applied the techniques of the social survey; a device, the possibilities of which, the librarian is just beginning to appreciate.

The advertiser is an interesting case for discussion here. The Institute of Practitioners in Advertising divides the audience into socioeconomic groups. It is assumed, on survey data, that there will be a difference of life style and educational attainment in each group and this difference will affect the products purchased by each group. Grade AB accounts for the upper professional and managerial classes. Grade C denotes the middle range professional and managerial classes. C2 denotes the supervisory technical grades, *ie* the 'artisan classes' so beloved of the Victorians. Grade DE, the manual labouring classes and old-age pensioners.

These grades are not put forward as being watertight or mutually exclusive, but they provide a communication base for the advertiser who wishes to advertise vintage sherry or motorbikes. The more serious point, however, is that the presentation of information differs in each of the newspapers which takes any of these socio-economic grades as its target audience. The presentation of information is very often a tug of war between the conscientious journalist who does not wish to simplify issues that are inherently complex, and the advertiser who is only interested in maximising his audience. Even public service television people succumb to the temptation to present information and news in the way that they imagine their audiences would like it. There is a growing volume of research to show that current affairs reporting is characterised by selectivity and an undue stress on negative events—the tragic things that happen in our society. As the media cynic said: 'Men on strike is news; men at work is not'.

The researches of Halloran (14) into demonstrations show that if guided by the selective and prejudiced eye, the camera is an accomplished deceiver in a way more insidious than print could ever be. The influence of social stereotypes and their effect on human attitudes is a crucial factor in the selction of news, particularly news from foreign countries. The main criteria in selection seem to be: the rank of the particular nation in the world hierarchy, the physical distance of the nation where the event happens and the degree to which the event fits in with the image of the particular country. News from South America tends to concentrate on revolutions in banana republics; news from Sweden tends to be about sexual license.

One important area in the information flow within society, where there is a need for expert reporting, is in the field of the popularisation of science. Television, which has such tremendous teaching potential, has on the whole been disappointing and, in the opinion of one scientist, has devoted itself to the sensationalising of scientific issues which are largely bogus. Since the launching of the first Russian satellite in 1957, the popular media have given greater emphasis to news of science than ever before. Space exploration, birth control, ecology, the social uses of automation, smoking and cancer—all these are key issues of our day; yet as Kriegbaum (15) points out, most of the vital decisions are left to the experts mainly because not enough people possess the background needed for a public airing of these issues.

There is an anecdote told of Benjamin Disraeli who, when he was informed how the development of communication was annihilating

177

distance between all parts of the globe, was alleged to have replied that the longest distance of all was the last two inches between a man's eyes and ears and his brain. In terms of the physical transporting of information from one area of the globe to another, the communications engineer could well turn to us and say: 'I have solved the technical problems, now get on with the job of communicating'. To a great extent his statement would be true. It is possible to arrange for the transmission of words and pictures from any point on the earth's surface to another. The communications satellite can transmit across ideological blocks, but there is no guarantee that the information will be accepted.

The social and economic gap that ever widens between the richer and poorer countries is also an information gap. To transplant a mass communications system into an underdeveloped country requires the support of a sophisticated technology and a trained personnel; both of which are outside the range of the poorer countries which comprise the so called third world. This term designates a region which according to the United Nations does not have a *per capita* income exceeding $300 per year. A third of the adults in the world cannot read or write; fifteen of the African countries have no newspaper (16). This problem provides a tremendous opportunity for librarianship; not as traditionally practiced, but as a systematic exploitation and dissemination of learning materials as a prerequisite to print literacy. As Lerner (17) points out the transistor radio was a greater success than either the book or the film because it made the minimum of cultural assumptions and by appealing to the ear was able to leap the literacy barrier.

As only the technologically rich countries can afford sophisticated media there is inevitably a centralisation of communication power and capacity. The International Telecommunications Satellite Consortium (INTELSTAT) represents the interests of 75 non-communist countries, but effective control of rates and operations lies in the hands of COMSAT the United States Communications Satellite Corporation. The problems of spreading the benefits of modern communications systems to the poorer countries, and the problems of comparative librarinaship, are basically similar and one of the objectives of this module might be to examine how one might assist the other.

8.5 MASS COMMUNICATIONS AND
INTERPERSONAL COMMUNICATION

In the foregoing sections I have dealt with the points of contact between empirical communications research and the librarian's interest in the information seeking behaviour of the individual. As I hopefully outlined in chapter two, the individual is not a passive entity existing in a social void; he is a social creature who derives his own self-esteem from the opinions of others. This, the last phase of the work leads us into a new area of enquiry called the Sociology of Knowledge. The idea that our knowledge is a social product is in some measure a study of recent interest. Its origins can be found in Marxist thought and its most elaborate statements in the work of Karl Mannheim (18). Not only is knowledge transmitted by the media of communication, but also by a lattice work of interpersonal communication. Brouwer (19), drawing on his research into the relationship between information and innovation in agricultural practice, makes the distinction between the getting of hard technical information for which farmers tended to rely on print, or electronic media, and the getting of grounds for a decision, where they are much more dependent on informal communications and are more subject to personal influence. He therefore constructs a model of the world of communications which he calls a 'mycelium model'. A mycelium is the complex underground network of the threads from which spring the mushroom. This underground network of informal communications leads to the 'mushroom', which can be compared with the products of the mass media of communication. They are all one system; but the formal communications are more dependent on the informal than vice versa. Without interpersonal communication there would be no mass communication.

Similarly within the field of knowledge published works are generally the result of many informal communications. One of the great and as yet unanswered questions imposed by the sociology of knowledge is: 'if knowledge is a social product, how can objective knowledge be possible?' When we speak of 'science', in the sense of endowing it with a special ontological status, are we merely speaking of the ideas, values and beliefs of scientists? They are men with similar interests who group together as a quasi-profession. Professions tend to form elites. Is science then what an elite of scientists happen to think at any particular time? One of the most fascinating and paradoxical points to emerge from the huge welter of empirical data is the ultimate dependence of our social system on the interpersonal mode of communication. Nowhere is this phenomenon more evident than in the system of the sciences. Although falsely objectified as a cold infallible reality beyond the ken of ordinary mortals, it is in fact a social system with all the norms and modes of social communication, and the same is true of all fields of knowledge. Ziman puts the point succinctly:

Beneath the surface layer of formal publication in science there exists many networks of informal communication. The old courtesies of private correspondence, the new vulgarities of conference and meetings, interchange of manuscripts and data, sabbatical leaves, consulting visits, seminars, conversations—these knit together the scholarly world in a way that is scarcely evident to the outsider (20).

One of the advantages which were instanced as a result of printing was the fact that scholars could remain sedentary and read; they did not need to travel as did the wandering scholars of medieval times. The wheel seems to have come round full circle: the telephone, air mail and particularly jet travel can bring the members of an 'invisible college' together much faster than the normal publication procedures. It would seem from the published literature on the subject that the inter-personal activity acts as a wave front of advancing knowledge, followed closely behind by the data storage systems which check and consolidate the position. The salient point for the student to grasp is that all areas of human knowledge involve people, and this logically entails a social system, and in all social systems there is a core area of consensus.

When a scientist writes a research paper he cites the work of his colleagues, but these citations not only serve to validate the claims he makes but they also embed the work in a pre-existing consensus. Like every other social being he seeks the esteem of his peers and superiors; and this esteem is often expressed in the coin of recognition accorded to his work by fellow-scientists. As individuals we are susceptible to the opinions of others especially in the formation of our own self-image. In the case of the scientists Storer (21) has shown that scientists who receive recognition early in their careers are more productive in later years than who do not. The 'gatekeeper' functions in the universe of the scientist just as he does in the communications system of the mass media. In science, as in every other institutional realm, a special problem of the reward system occurs when individuals or organisations take up the task of gauging performances on behalf of the larger community. The referee of a scientific journal is an example of this problem. As a social being he is likely to be influenced by the stereotype of the person presenting the contribution. If he is famous, there is a greater chance of his contribution being accepted for publication and his views gaining a hearing from his colleagues. As Merton (22) observes , eminent scientists get disproportionately greater credit for their contributions to science, while relatively little known scientists tend to get disproportionately less credit for comparable contributions. He calls this the 'Matthew effect': 'For unto everyone that hath shall be given, and he shall have abundance.' (23)

The same principle applies to the development of communications system in the poorer countries, who have extreme difficulty in ever getting to the 'take-off' point; while the knowledge industry in the richer nations increases at the now familiar exponential rate. The study of the communications systems in both the sciences and the social sciences seem to contradict the cherished assumptions of traditional library school teaching. The accepted dogma was that abstracts gave an inestimable service by enabling the scientist to read quickly and keep abreast of his field, whilst performing the economy of avoiding duplication of research effort. Studies of the reading practices of scientists would seem to indicate that the phrase 'no one reads it' is by no means an exaggeration. Achoff (24) and Halbert assert that about one per cent of the articles published in journals of chemistry are read by any one chemist, and much the same pattern has been found in the behavioural sciences (25).

The conclusion would seem to be that the social institution responsible for the growth of scientific knowledge, or indeed knowledge in any discipline is the 'invisible college': a small group of highly productive specialists who, sharing the same field of study, communicate with one another, and monitor the progress in their field. Diana Crane (26), a sociologist, has shown that research areas within basic science go through the same stages of slow growth, exponential growth, linear growth and gradual decline, that have been identified in science as a whole. Scientists are attracted to a research area by interesting discoveries that provide models for future work. A few highly productive scientists get priorities for research, recruit and train students and communicate with other members within their area. The activities of this 'invisible college' produce a period of exponential growth in publications and provide the driving force for the development of the new subject. It is, therefore, no abstract field moving under its own impetus, but is like all social systems having powerful elites who determine what the objectives shall be, how they shall be accomplished and who shall communicate with whom. Knowledge, society and communication are, like theologians used to assert of the Trinity: one and indivisible.

8.6 COMMUNICATIONS AND THE BOOK

In this, the last section, we shall examine the place of the book as a medium of information transfer and its future role in the context of other forms of communication. The book as we know it today has been a significant phenomenon for only a relatively short period of history, and it is a medium which has continually changed its form to adapt to new circumstance. The book on the monastery lectern differs from the book of the seventeenth century and from the paper-back of our own time. Like other forms of publication it has been an integral part of the knowledge explosion. In the centuries before Gutenberg there had been approximately 30,000 new titles and editions of books produced in Europe. In the 150 years up to the year 1600 there were 40,000 new titles. From 1600 to 1700 there were 1.25 million new titles; from 1700 to 1800 there were 2 million. Exponential growth of recorded knowledge has been with us ever since. The content of books from the fall of Rome to the seventeenth century were largely philosophical and theological; the book was envisaged mainly as a work of reference. Like the library it assumes a whole host of social, technological and economic factors; the book requires also the conjunction of the distinct possibilities of production marketing and readership. According to George Steiner there was a classic phase in the history of the book when it was a privately owned object. It was the age of the private library, of privacy and freedom from the competition of rival distractions—the key requirements of space and silence.

A man sitting in his library is at once the inheritor and the begetter of a particular social and moral order. It is a bourgeois order founded on certain hierarchies of literacy purchasing power, of leisure and of caste. (27)

The very ideas which shattered this social and moral order gave a new direction to the form and content of the book. People needed literacy and the book, in order to secure a higher degree of control over their own lives and destinies. In other words, the struggle for more books was involved in the struggle for more political and economic freedom.

As we have seen in chapter six, the technological developments in the printing and paper industry transformed the whole nature of publishing. The factory production of paper made by machinery, and the mechanical printing and rotary press, formed the necessary basis for the mass production of books. By the middle of the nineteenth century books had become a commodity and the publishing trade had become an industry worthy of investment. The machinery, and the entrepreneurial flair which was discussed in chapter seven provided the capital. During the first half of the nineteenth century books, as distinct from broadsheets, magazines and penny issues, were still too expensive for the poor to buy. *Mansfield park* cost eighteen shillings, nearly three times the wages of an agricultural labourer even had he the necessary leisure, lighting and privacy from the noise and squalor of his family (28).

By the 1840's, prices had dropped and new cheap editions, 'yellow backs' or 'railway libraries' were introduced. From then on the rise in book production increased sharply; by 1850 two thousand books were published, by 1901 6,000 and by 1914 this figure had doubled. We can compare this with the present situation by checking on the numbers of new titles published each year. Although we have few libraries in private apartments, and our personal space and leisure time is crowded by competing activities, the making of books has not yet reached its end. The expansion of higher education has been an important factor in this. The modern paperback is a brilliant example of how the book can adapt to changing social parameters. It is compact, it can be put in a handbag or the back pocket and used in casual and fragmented circumstances.

Democracy of access is evident as we see Sophocles and Mickey Spillane on the same bookrack in the local bookshop. The book, as McLuhan has deplored, still demands withdrawal from others—itself a socially hostile act. Yet this demand for a temporary private world is only apparent, for the book exemplified what we said about concepts, and networks of human relationships: books are in large measure about previous books. But what of other media? How will they affect the future of the book?

Many of the newer media have served to stimulate the use of

books. When television first became popular it was regarded as inimical to the book and many respectable journals in librarianship were given to discussing this problem. But is was a pseudo-problem: the coming of broadcasting in 1922 and the postwar spurt in television both accompanied a rise in book lending. There is of course a logical flaw in asserting that because A and B both happen together that there is a causal relationship between them. As Cherry (29) notes in discussing the growth curves in booklending, there is a danger in attaching too great a precision when there are other factors to take into account, such as the increase in educational facilities and the growth of population. It can be demonstrated that the period of greatest growth took place in the twenty five years after the war and Huse (30) marshals statistics to show this:

POPULATION		BOOK ISSUES
1946	48 million	287 million
1960	52 million	460 million
1969	54 million	600 million
Population growth: 12%		Growth of book issue: over 100%

The study of the way in which television has influenced libraries is a useful exercise in sociological analysis for the student. It should not however obscure the basic question which is: 'What is the nature of the *reading act* as compared with television viewing, listening to the radio or engaging in conversation with another person?' Very little attention has been paid by the profession to the psychology of the reading act and the various theories that have been put forward as to its nature. One of the basic errors in McLuhan's classification of the psychological effects of the media was the description of the reading process as *linear*, as against the multi-sensory act of watching television. The eye does not advance letter by letter along a line of type like a regimented guardsman. Helen Robinson (31) suggests that there are four phases in the reading process: perception, comprehension, reaction, assimilation. These stages are not strictly sequential but more or less simultaneous having indistinct and overlapping boundaries. The reading act is very much an act of perception and as such involves two simultaneous processes: scanning and integration.

Psychologists like Venezky (32) and Calfee have moved away from the traditional concept of letters and words, a conception which probably influenced McLuhan. There is the preliminary dance of the eye while the reader scans ahead testing whether the text will fulfil his expectations. As he scans, he integrates material into his 'temporary knowledge store' and then into the 'integrated knowledge store'. What the reader is looking for in his forward scanning is what Venezky calls the 'largest manageable unit', which will enable him to form appropriate patterns of meaning with what he already knows about the subject. The eye can dance back to re-assess and take in material which it feels will make the patterns more meaningful.

The book it portable and infinitely patient; it can be taken up and put down again. The necessity to 'playback' the winning goal, at length *ad nauseam* shows that television is a linear medium. But if the document gives, it also demands. The prime demand is prolonged contact and reasonable physical conditions—this latter requirement is of no mean importance. This applies to reading for information and reading for pleasure. Because of this, it draws the reader into a personalised, critical, and active state of mind. As I have mentioned in the foregoing sections the re-discovery of the importance of the interpersonal has been one of the significant features of contemporary media research.

Inter-personal communication, although it draws on and expands the latent warmth in the human personality, is unstructured and fleeting. More seriously still, it gives less time for reflection and diminishes the chance of a deep and critical response. Wise committees, when faced with enthusiastic oratory from a member on a new proposal, usually request the presentation of a paper setting out a structured and reasoned argument. The great benefit of interpersonal communication is that it gives man the psychological benefits of the tribal community; but librarians, above all others, should be watchful of the concomitant dangers.

The tribal situation, for all its emotional security, was a tyrannical one; and the great tyrants of history were often persuasive orators. The etymology of the word 'dictator' means one who speaks without interruption; and there is no reason why the mass media should not serve to make tyranny the more effective because they make the oral mode of communication more powerful. Gerry Smith (34) in a well-argued paper, asserts that the role of the public library should be to act as an agency of scrutiny, and to complement the mass media in the treatment of current affairs. They can do this by providing a wide range of primary documents, and the material produced by involved pressure groups, to give detailed first hand information on social, economic and political problems of contemporary concern. The surveys conducted by James Curran (34) showed that, even though people like to watch the television news, they still like to read an account in the newspaper where they can critically examine the arguments presented and form their own conclusions.

The domination of print in western society not only made possible the technological efficiency of that society but created the conditions of freedom and democratic government, and although the electronic media have, as McLuhan suggests, tended to re-create the conditions of a pre-literate culture there is no necessity for us to go round the circle of history again. Northrop Frye, the Canadian literary critic (36), encapsulates this danger in a phrase that all librarians should note; and it provides a thought-provoking quotation with which to conclude this book:

Democracy and book culture are interdependent and the rise of oral and visual media represents, not a new order to adjust to, but a subordinate order to be contained.

8.7 CONCLUSION AND SUMMARY

This assertion of Professor Frye's has far-reaching implications not only for the quality of social life but also for the purpose and philosophy of librarianship. The foregoing chapters have dealt with how man acquires and stores information; how he seeks to find out and the way in which he is influenced by others in his communication behaviour. They have outlined the interrelationships and reciprocal influences between technology and human behaviour and attempted to isolate the consequences for libraries and librarianship. But user studies and information technology are not ends in themselves; they are only *instrumental* in the furtherance of human understanding and the constant revivifying of the human imagination: qualities which are necessary for a stable and compassionate society. Librarianship depends upon technology and upon the behavioural sciences; the former to save time and costs, the latter to acquire an interpretive understanding of how human beings think, believe and behave as they do. But if the ultimate concern of librarianship ends here then we are guilty of having a very Benthamite view of man, reducing men and women to consumers of units of information, subject to analysis by computers and to

186

analysis as data in social surveys. Its ultimate end is not to acquire, store and disseminate information simply that man may accumulate knowledge at the expense of understanding and imagination. The book that Northrop Frye has in mind is the 'literary book' which has not been dealt with in the course of this work but fields of knowledge outlined in the foregoing chapters can hopefully be put forward as a prolegomena to the appreciation of the critical reading of a literary text. We know so very little about this communication encounter except to infer from our own experience that it demands imagination, critical ability and self-discipline, qualities which help to make 'democratic man'. Such reading requires imaginative identification with the author's intent and the ability to detach oneself from one's own point of view. Life is short and we have to allocate our reading time distracted by competing activities and pursuits. Books differ from one another; the values in *Mein Kampf* differ from those in Thomas A Kempis's *Imitation of Christ* and we have the freedom to make a choice. Some books demand more, others less: Henry James is more exacting in what he required from his readers than, say, Georgette Heyer. The critical reading of works of the imagination call for a certain degree of self-abnegation and since we are all inclined to be lazy it is often tempting to sink back passively into the oozy warmth of the mass culture provided by the mass media. The problem with freedom and democracy is that they require active participation hence Frye's admonition on keeping the audio-visual media within bounds. Another implication lies in the traditional classifications of knowledge. Thomas de Quincey distinguished the 'literature of knowledge' from what he called the 'literature of power' (33). The former encompasses those books concerned with facts and information, as commonly understood. The 'literature of power' connotes those books which express rather than inform: books from which the reader may learn nothing but by which he may become something. But the more we consider this division the more we contemplate the fatuity of rigidly demarcating the products of reason and imagination; fact and fiction as we have traditionally done. The novel may be a source of knowledge even though its arrangement may be different from that of the conventional textbook. We can get invaluable insights into human behaviour by reading William Golding's *The lord of the flies* as well as by reading a textbook on child psychology or group dynamics. There are few texts on developmental psychology that cannot be enhanced by the reading of Wordsworth's *Prelude* where the way in which the mind develops is registered with such delicacy and acuteness of observation. Both literature and the behavioural sciences complement each other. The behavioural sciences deal with general ideas, they teach us about people in abstract categories which we endeavour to apply in our professional and private relationships. The novelist, dramatist or poet also has a general and universal conception of man but the treatment is usually concrete and individual; the work contains a distillation of the creator's own experience and apprehension of reality. Curricula in librarianship have become increasingly conscious (34) of the problems of the social context and ingenious in adapting technological aids to professional skills but it would be a pity if we neglected the life of the spirit by relegating the humanities to a subordinate position as though we were ashamed of something simply because it cannot be measured. There may be more of a humanistic purpose in librarianship than we had originally suspected.

1 Harold Lasswell 'The structure and function of communication in society' *in* L Bryson *Communications of ideas* New York, Harper, 1948, p 48.

2 Theodore Peterson and others *The mass media and modern society* New York, Holt, Rinehart and Winston, 1965.

3 S G Berryman 'Bringing town and country together' *Library Association Conference Proceedings* Brighton, 1972.

4 O N Larsen 'The social effects of mass communication' *in* R L Faris *Handbook of modern sociology* New York, Rand McNally, 1966.

5 Lowell Martin *Library response to urban change* Chicago, ALA, 1969.

6 B H Baumfield 'The new seekers: study of the work of the public libraries research group' *Library Association record* 75 (8) August 1973, p 150-52.

7 Results due to be published in 1974.

8 Institute of Practitioners in Advertising *Readership surveys.*

9 Elihu Katz *and* Paul Lazarfield *Personal influence: the part played by the people in the flow of mass communications* New York, Free Press, 1965.

10 Leon Festinger *Theory of cognitive dissonance* Evancton (111) Row, Peterson, 1957.

11 Brian Abel Smith *The poor and the poorest* London, Bell, 1965. For the problems in the United States see also R G Chester 'Information in the health care system' in *Annals of the American Academy of Political and Social Science* 412, March 1974, p 138-44.

12 Malcolm Warner *The data bank society: organisations, computers and social freedom* London, Allen & Unwin, 1972.

13 Kurt Lewin 'Channels of group life' in *Human relationships* 1 (2) 1947, p 143-53.

14 James Halloran *Demonstrations and communications* London, Penguin Books, 1971.

15 Hillier Kriegbaum *Science and the mass media* London, University of London Press, 1968.

16 John Soupham *Revolution in communications* New York, Holt, 1971.

17 Daniel Lerner *Passing of traditional society: modernizing the Middle East*
New York, Free Press, 1968.

18 Karl Mannheim *Essays in the sociology of knowledge* London, Toutledge
and Kegan Paul, 1936.

19 M Brouwer 'Prolegomena to the study of mass communication' *in*
L Thayer editor *Communications: concepts and perspective* Washington, Spartan
Books, 1966.

20 J Ziman *Public knowledge* Cambridge, Cambridge University Press, 1960,
p 108.

21 Norman Storer *The social system of science* New York, Holt, Rinehart,
1966.

22 R K Merton 'The Matthew effect in science' in *Science* 159 (2) 1967, p 56-
63.

23 St Matthew's gospel.

24 *R L Ackoff and M H Halbert An operational research study of the scientific
activity of chemists* Case Institute of Technology. Operations Research Group
(Cleveland) 1958.

25 *W J Paisley The flow of behavioural science information* Stanford
University: Institute for Communications Research, 1966.

25.1 *European journal of sociology* 4: 1963: 237

26 Colin Cherry *World communications threat or promise* New York:
Wiley, 1971.

27 Roy J Huse *Communication and information* Chichester: Barry, Rose,
1974 For world statistics on book production and distribution see Robert
Escarpit and R Barker *The book hunger*. UNESCO/HARROP, 1974.

28 Helen Robinson *Reading* Chicago University Press, 1966.

29 Richard Venesky *and* Robert Calfee. A reading competency model *in*
H Shiger, *ed Theoretical problems and processes of reading* Newark
(Delaware): International Reading Association, 1971, p. 277 see also the
collection of essays by my colleague A W McClellan *The reader the book*
Bingley, 1973.

30 Gerry Smith 'The documentation of current affairs in public libraries'
Library Association record 79: (9): September, 1971.

31 James Curran 'The impact of television on the reading of newspapers' *in*
Jeremy Tunstall ed *Media Sociology* London: Constable, 1971.

32 Northrop Frye 'Communications' *The Listener* 87 9 July, 1970, p. 5.
Similar themes are explored from an existentialist viewpoint in Ronald
Benge's *Communication and identity* London: Clive Bingley, Hamden,
Conn. Linnet Books, 1972.

33 Thomas de Quincey 'Letters to a young man whose education has been
neglected' *London Magazine* 2. 1823. There is an extended treatment of this and
related themes in Holbrook Jackson's *The reading of books*. London, Faber, 1946.

34 *see* Roger Poole 'The affirmation is of life: the later criticism of
F R Leavis' *Universities quarterly* 29,1 Winter 1974, pp 60–90.

SELECT BIBLIOGRAPHY FOR FURTHER READING

Chapter 1

ASHBY, W R: *Introduction to cybernetics*. London: Methuen, 1956.

BENGE, R C: *Communication and identity*. London: Bingley, Hamden, Conn: Linnet Books, 1972.

BERGEN, Daniel: 'Implications of general systems theory for librarianship and higher education' *in College and Research Libraries* 27: (5): 1966: 358-88.

BERLO, David K: *The process of communication*. New York: Holt, Rinehart and Winston, 1960.

BURR, Robert L: 'Libraries and librarianship: a model' *in Libri*: January, 1974.

DEUTSCH, Karl: 'Knowledge in the growth of civilizations' *in* Montgomery, E B, *editor: Foundations of access to knowledge*. Syracuse: University Press, 1968.

FANO, R M: 'Information theory and the retrieval of recorded information' *in* Shera, Jesse *Documentation in action*. New York: Reinhold, 1956.

FEIBLEMAN, James: 'Integrative levels in nature' *in* Kyle, Barbara, *editor: Focus on information and communication*. London: Aslib, 1965.

FLOOD, Merrill: 'Systems approach to library planning' *in Library quarterly* 34: (4): 1964: 326-8.

FOSKETT, D J: 'Information and general system theory' *in Journal of Librarianship* 4: (3): July, 1972: 205-09.

GOFFMAN, W: 'A general theory of communication' *in* Saracevik, T *editor: Introduction to information science*. New York: Bowker, 1970.

GORDON, N: *The languages of communication*. New York: Hastings House, 1967.

LERNER, Daniel: *Parts and wholes*. New York: MacMillan, 1963.

MATSON, Floyd *and* MONTAGUE, Ashley: *The human dialogue*. New York: Free Press, 1967.

MILLER, George: *The psychology of communication*. Harmondsworth: Free Press, 1967.

MOODY, M: 'The librarian as communication analyst' *in AHIL Quarterly* 9: Fall, 1967: 14-18.

NEILL, S D: 'Contact factor'. *Canadian Library Journal* 30: January, 1973: 48-64.

NITECKI, J Z: 'Towards a conceptual pattern in librarianship'.

General Systems Bulletin 11:(11):June, 1970:2-16.

SCHAFFER, Dale E: *The maturity of librarianship as a profession.* Metuchen (NJ): Scarecrow Press, 1968.

SETHI, A R: 'Communication in libraries' *in Herald of Library Science* 11: January, 1972: 43-52.

SHERA, Jesse: *Foundations of education for librarianship.* New York: Becker and Hayes, 1971.

VAGIANOS, L: 'The problem of 'noise'' *in Library Journal* 97: October, 1972: 3289-91.

WEINER, Norbert: *God and golem inc.: a comment on certain points where cybernetics impinges on religion.* Cambridge (Mass): MIT Press, 1964.

YOUNG, M F D: *Knowledge and control.* London: Collier-MacMillan, 1971.

ZIMAN, J: 'New lamps for old: lights of knowledge' *Aslib Proceedings* 22: May, 1970: 186-200.

Chapter 2

ARANGUREN, J L: *Human communication.* London: Weidenfeld and Nicholson, 1967.

ARGYLE, Michael: *Psychology of interpersonal relations.* Harmondsworth (Middlx): Penguin Books, 1968.

BECHTEL, A A: 'The problem of communication' *in Drexel Library Quarterly* 1: January, 1965: 37-50.

BERRY, D: 'Communication and the librarian' *in Utah Libraries:* Fall 1969: 12-18.

CHASE, Stuart: *Danger—men talking,* New York: Parents Magazine Press, 1970.

DOUGLAS, Mary: *Natural symbols: explorations in cosmology.* London: Barrie and Rockliff, 1968.

EHLERS, A S: 'The role of the library in the communication process'. *South African Libraries* 39: December 1971: 178-85.

FIRTH, Raymond: *Symbols public and private.* London: Allen and Unwin, 1973.

FOSKETT, D J: 'Language and classification' *in Journal of Documentation* 21: December, 1965: 285-88.

GARDIN, J C: 'Document analysis and linguistic theory' *in Journal of Documentation* 29: (6): 1973.

GELLERMAN, S W: *The management of human relations.* New York: Holt, Rinehart and Winston, 1966.

GERARD, David E *editor: Public libraries and the arts.* London: Bingley, Hamden, Conn: Linnet Books, 1970.

GURVITCH, Georges: *The social framework of knowledge.* Oxford: Blackwell, 1971.

HEAD, M C: 'Bridged any good gaps lately?' *in SLA News* 106: November-December, 1971: 392-6.

JACOBSON, T E: 'The library as a cultural centre' *in Anglo-Scandinavian Conference Proceedings.* 1970. Helsinki: Finnish Library Association, 1971.

KOCHEN, Manfred: 'World information system and encyclopaedia' *in Journal of Documentation* 28: December, 1972: 322-43.

LEE, Brian: 'What does linguistics mean?' *in Use of English* 24: (4): Summer, 1973: 367-73.

McKAY, Donald: *Information and meaning.* Cambridge (Mass): MIT Press, 1969.

MINNIS, Noel *editor: Linguistics at large.* London: Gollancz, 1971.

MORRIS, Charles: *Signs, language and behaviour.* New York: Brazillier, 1946.

NASH, Walter: *Our experience of language.* London: Batsford, 1971.

PEARS, David: *What is knowledge?* London: Allen and Unwin, 1972.

REISER, Oliver: *The integration of human knowledge.* Boston: Sargent, 1968.

SAUNDERS, W: 'Development of libraries as a key factor in communication', *in Library Association Conference Proceedings 1971 Blackpool.* London: Library Association, 1972.

SCHON, Donald: *Beyond the stable state: public and private learning in a changing society.* London: Temple-Smith, 1971.

SHERA, Jesse: *Libraries and the organization of knowledge.* London: Crosby Lockwood, 1965.

idem. 'Sociological relationships of information science' *in Journal of the American Society for Information Science* 22: (2): March 1971: 76-80.

SMITH, Alfred G: *Communication and culture: readings in the code of human interaction.* New York: Holt, Kinenart & Winston, 1965.

SWANSON, Don: 'Information business is people business'. *Information Storage and Retrieval* 6: October, 1970: 35-61

ULLMANN, Stephen: *Semantics: an introduction to the science of meaning*. New York: Barnes and Noble, 1962.

VIAUD, Graston: *Intelligence: its evolution and forms*. London: Hutchinson, 1960.

WATSON, L E *and others:* 'Sociology and information science' *in Journal of librarianship* 5: (4): 1973: 270-84.

WHITE, Leslie A: *The evolution of culture*. New York: McGraw Hill, 1959.

ZIMAN, J: 'Information communication and knowledge'. *in Nature* 224: 25 October, 1969: 318-24.

ZNANIECKI, Florian: *The social role of the man of knowledge* New York: Columbia University Press, 1940.

Chapter 3

BELOFF, J: 'Creative thinking in arts and science' *in British journal of aesthetics* 10: 1970: 58-70.

BROOKS, B C: 'Jesse Shera and the theory of bibliography' *Journal of librarianship* 5: (4): October, 1973.

BUTLER, Pierce: *The reference function of the library*. Chicago: Chicago University Press, 1942.

CRUM, M J: 'The librarian—customer relationship' *in Special libraries* 60: (5): May, 1969: 269-77.

FRANCIS, *Sir* Frank: 'The two cultures in information work' *in Aslib proceedings* 20: June, 1968: 268-88.

FREIDES, T: 'Will the real reference problems please stand up?' *in Library journal* 91: (8): April, 1966: 2008-12.

HARGREAVES, David: *Interpersonal relations and education*. London: Routledge and Kegan Paul, 1972.

JONES, K H: 'Creative library management: the limiting factors' *in Assistant librarian* 66: (10): October, 1973: 158-65.

MARTIN, Lowell: *The library response to urban change*. Chicago: ALA, 1969.

MEERLOO, Joost M: *Conversation and communication*. New York: International Universities Press, 1952.

MILLER, G A: 'Psychology and information' *in American documentation* 19: July, 1968: 286-9.

OATES, J F: 'Levels of interaction between man and information' *in American documentation* 19: July, 1968: 290-4.

PENLAND, Patrick: *The floating librarian*. Pittsburgh University of Pittsburgh Library School, 1970.

SPENCE, A C: *Management communication: process and practice.*

London: MacMillan, 1969.
THAYER, Lee, *editor: Communication and communication systems.* Homewood (Illinois): Irwin, 1968.
VAVREK, Bernard: *Communications and the reference interface.* Ann Arbor (Michigan): University Microfilms, 1971.
WATZLAWICK, Paul, *and others: Pragmatics of human communication.* London: Faber, 1968.

Chapter 4
ARGYLE, Michael: *Non-verbal communication.* Oxford: Blackwell, 1973.
BERRY, D: 'Communication and the librarian'. *Utah libraries,* Fall, 1969: 12-18.
BIRDWHISTELL, J L: *Kinesics and context.* Pennsylvania: University of Pennsylvania Press, 1970.
DALY, J E: *Organizing non-print materials.* New York: Dekker, 1972.
EISENBERGER, A M *and* SMITH, R: *Non-verbal communication.* New York: Bobbs-Merrill, 1971.
ENGLER, M C: 'Message versus machine' *in Catholic library world* 44: (8): March, 1973.
FOTHERGILL, Richard: *A challenge for librarians.* London: National Council for Educational Technology, 1971.
GINGRICH, A: 'Communications media and people' *in Illinois libraries* 51: April, 1967: 132-47.
GOFFMAN, Erving: *The presentation of self in everyday life.* New York: Anchor books, 1959.
HALL, E T: *Hidden dimension.* New York: Doubleday, 1966.
HARE, G: 'Resource centres: a challenge to the library service'. *Library Association Conference Proceedings 1971.* Blackpool, 1972.
HINDE, Robert: *Non-verbal communication.* London: Cambridge University Press, 1971.
IVENS, William: *Prints and visual communication.* London: Routledge and Kegan Paul, 1953.
MATTHEWS, K: 'Communication in children's services in public libraries'. *Illinois libraries* 55: (1): January, 1973: 2-8.
MIRO, G *and* HAZING, J: *Communication in art architecture printing and music.* Denver: University of Chicago, 1962.
REID, L A: *Ways of knowledge and experience.* London: Allen and Unwin, 1961.

194

SHOSID, N J: 'Freud, frug and feedback: am I communicating?' *in Special libraries* 57: October, 1966: 561-3

SMITH, D: 'Matters of confidence: how reference librarians handle an enquiry' *in Library journal* 97: (7) April, 1972.

TAYLOR, L C: *Resources for learning.* 2nd ed. Harmondsworth (Middlx): Penguin Books, 1972.

Chapter 5

BIGGS, J R: *The story of the alphabet.* London: Oxford University Press, 1968.

BRITISH MUSEUM: *Writing in Western Asia: origin and development from pictures to letters.* London: British Museum, 1970. (Slides).

CAHN, W: *Story of writing from cave art to computer.* New York: Harvey, 1963.

CONDIT, Lester: 'Bibliography in its pre-natal existence' *in Library quarterly* 7: 1937: 546-76.

DOWNING, J G: *Story of language and writing.* London: Wheaton, 1967.

FABRE, Maurice: *History of communications.* New York: Hawthorn Books, 1965.

FIORE, S: *Voices from the clay: Assyro-Babylonian culture.* Oklahoma: Norman, 1965.

GELB, I F: *The study of writing.* Chicago: Chicago University Press, 1963.

GUPPY, Henry: 'Human records: a survey of their history from the beginnings' *in John Rylands Library* 27: 1942: 182-222.

HAVELOCK, R: *Preface to Plato.* Cambridge: Harvard University Press, 1965.

HOOKE, S M: 'The early history of writing' *in Antiquity* 5: (2): 1937: 261-77.

INNIS, Harold: 'Communications and archaeology' *in Journal of economics and political science* 17: May 1957: 237-50.

LORD, Albert: *Singers of tales.* Cambridge (Mass): Harvard University Press, 1964.

MUNBY, F A: *Publishing and bookselling: a history from the earliest times to the present.* London: Cape, 1949.

NEAL, H E: *Communications from stone age to space age.* London: Phoenix House, 1960.

NICHOLAS, Charles: *The library of Rameses the Great.* Berkeley:

California University Press, 1964.

REDFIELD, Robert: *The primitive world and its transformations.* Cornell University Press, 1953.

SMITH, Josephine: *Chronology of librarianship.* New York: Scarecrow Press, 1968.

ULLMANN, B L: *Ancient writing and its influence.* London: Longmans, 1932.

Chapter 6

ALLEN, Francis: *Technology and social change.* New York: Appleton-Century-Croft. 1957.

BENNETT, H S: *English books and readers 1603-1640.* London: Cambridge University Press, 1970.

CARLSON, W M: 'Communications technology and the library of the future' *PLA bulletin*: 24: January 1959: 5-14.

CARTER, J *and* MUIR, P: *Printing and the mind of man.* London: Cassell, 1967.

CIPOLLA, C M: *Literacy and development in the West.* Harmondsworth (Middlex): Penguin Books, 1969.

GOODY, Jack: *Literacy in traditional societies.* London: Cambridge University Press, 1969.

HEER, Friedrich: *The medieval world.* London: Weidenfeld and Nicholson, 1969.

JENNETT, Sean: *The making of books.* New York: Praeger, 1967.

LERNER, Daniel: *The passing of traditional society.* Glencoe (Illinois) Free Press, 1958.

McLUHAN, Marshall: *The Gutenberg galaxy.* Toronto: Toronto University Press, 1965.

McMURTRIE, Douglas: *The book: the story of printing and bookmaking.* London: Oxford University Press, 1942.

MERTON, R K: *Science, technology and society in seventeenth century England.* New York: Harper and Row, 1938.

MILLER, Jonathan: *Marshall McLuhan.* London: Collins, 1971.

MUMFORD, Lewis: *Technics and civilization.* New York: Harcourt Brace and World, 1963.

TAWNEY, R H: *Religion and the rise of capitalism.* Harmondsworth (Middlx): Penguin Books, 1946.

THOMPSON, J W: *The medieval library.* Chicago: Chicago University Press, 1939.

WHITE, Lynn: *Medieval technology and social change.* New York:

Oxford University Press, 1966.

WORMALD, Francis: *The English library before 1800*. London: University of London Press, 1958.

Chapter 7

BELL, Daniel: *The end of ideology*. New York: Collier MacMillan, 1961.

BLUM, E: *Basic books in the mass media*. 2nd ed. Urbana: Illinois University Press, 1973.

CARTER, E F: 'Communications in a complex world' *in Special libraries* 52: October, 1967: 445-8.

CARTER, Martin: *An introduction to mass communications*. London: MacMillan, 1971.

CHERRY, Colin: *World communications: threat or promise: a socio-technical approach*. New York: Wiley, 1970.

CONANT, R W: *The public library and the city*. Cambridge (Mass): MIT Press, 1964.

DRUCKER, Peter: *Technology management and society*. London: Pan Books, 1969.

ELLERTING, J: 'The sociology of libraries and their publics' *in Libri*: 16: (2): 87-112.

ENNIS, P: 'The library consumer patterns and trends' *in Library quarterly* 34: April, 1964: 163: 78.

FESBACH, Seymour *and* SINGER, Robert: *Television and aggression*. San Francisco: Jossey-Bass, 1971.

FOSKETT, D J: 'Intellectual and social challenge of the library service' *in Library Association record* 70: December, 1968: 305-9.

GOODE, W: 'The librarian from occupation to profession' *in Library quarterly* 31: 1961: 306-18.

HALMOS, Paul: *The personal service society*. London: Constable, 1970.

HANSENS, Donald A *and* PARSONS, J H: *Mass communication: a research bibliography*. Santa Barbara (Calif): Glendessary Press, 1969.

KELLY, Thomas: *History of the public library in Britain 1845-1965*. London: Library Association, 1973.

KORNHANSER, W: *The politics of mass society*. London: Routledge and Kegan Paul, 1960.

LASSWELL, H D: 'Policy problems of a data rich civilization' *in Wilson Library bulletin*. 41: Summer 1966: 58-65.

LUCKHAM, B L and ORR, J: 'Broadcasting and the public libraries, *in Library Association record*: January, 1967: 11-13.

McLUHAN, Marshall: *Understanding media*. London: Routledge and Kegan Paul, 1964.

McQUAIL, Denis: *Towards a sociology of the mass media*. London: Collier-MacMillan, 1969.

MARTIN, A B: *Strategy for public library change*. Chicago: ALA, 1972.

MEIER, Richard: 'Communications overload proposals from the study of a university library' *in Administrative science quarterly* 7: 1962/3: 521-44.

MUNFORD, W A: *Penny rate: aspects of British public library history*. London: The Library Association, 1951.

PETERSEN, Theodore: 'Mass media and public enlightenment' *in Illinois libraries* 49: March, 1967: 149-58.

PETERSEN, Theodore *and others: The mass media and modern society*. New York: Holt, Rinehart and Winston, 1965.

RAWSKI, Conrad, *editor: Towards a theory of librarianship*. Metuchen, (NJ) Scarecrow Press, 1973.

SAUNDERS, W L: *Libraries in an age of communication*. Library Association Conference Proceedings, 1972.

SCHRAMM, Wilbur: *The process and effects of mass communication* 2nd ed. Urbana (Ill) University of Illinois Press, 1970.

WORSLEY, Peter: 'Libraries and mass culture' *in Library Association record*: 69: August, 1967: 259-67.

WRIGHT, C R: *Mass communications: a sociological perspective*. New York: Random House, 1959.

YATES, B: 'Role of the technological gatekeeper' *in Aslib Proceedings* 22: October, 1970: 57-110.

Chapter 8

ASHWORTH, Wilfred: 'The information explosion' *in Library Association record*, 76:4 April 1974.

BAGDIKIAN, Ben H: *The information machines: their impact on men and media*. New York: Harper and Row, 1971.

BARKER, A: *The member of parliament and his information*. London: Allen & Unwin, 1970.

BERGER, Peter L *and* LUCKMANN, Thomas: *The social construction of reality: a treatise in the sociology of knowledge*. London: Allen Lane, Penguin Press, 1969.

BRIGGS, Asa: *The history of broadcasting in the United Kingdom.* London: Oxford University Press, 1962-70. 3v.

BROWN, J A C: *Techniques of persuasion.* Harmondsworth (Middlx) Penguin Books: 1963.

DOOB, Leonard W: *Communication in Africa: a search for boundaries.* New Haven (Conn): Yale University Press, 1961.

DOVE, J: 'Libraries and local radio' *in Assistant librarian*: 64: July 1971: 56-8.

EDWARDS, Donald: *Local radio.* London: BBC, 1969.

GANN, Peter D: 'Data banks and readership surveys' *in Assistant Librarian*: Sept 1971: 130-3.

GOFFMANN, W *and* NEVILL, V A: 'Communication and epidemic processes' *in Proceedings of the Royal Society.* 298: 1967: 316-334.

GREENBERG, Bradley S *and* DERVIN, Brenda: *The use of the mass media by the urban poor.* New York: Praeger, 1970.

HOLLIDAY, Leslie: *The integration of technologies.* London: Hutchinson, 1966.

HOLROYD, Gileon: 'Sociology of knowledge'. *in Journal of librarianship*: 4: (1) January, 1972: 18-23.

JOUVENAL, Bertrand de: *The art of conjecture.* London: Weidenfeld and Nicholson, 1967.

KATZ, Elihu *and* LAZARFELD, Paul: *Personal influence: the part played by people in the flow of mass communications.* Glencoe (Ill) Free Press, 1955.

KATZ, Elihu: 'The two step flow of communication' *in Public opinion quarterly* 21: 1957: 61-8.

LAMBERTON, D M, *editor: Economics of information and knowledge.* Harmondsworth (Middlx): Penguin Books, 1971.

LEE, John, *editor: Diplomatic persuaders: new role of the mass radio in international relations.* New York: Wiley, 1968.

LICKLIDER, J C R: *Libraries of the future.* Cambridge (Mass): MIT Press, 1965.

MERTON, R K: *Social theory and social structure.* Glencoe, Free Press, 1957.

PAISLEY, William: *The flow of behavioural science information.* Stanford University: Institute for Communication Research, 1966.

PARKER, E B: 'The effects of television on public library circulation' *in Public opinion quarterly* 27: 1963: 570-88.

PETERSON, T: 'Mass media and public enlightenment' *in Illinois*
199

libraries: 49: March, 1967: 149-58.

SCUPHAM, John: *The revolution in communications*. London: Holt, Rinehart and Winston, 1970.

SEYMOUR-URE, Colin: *The press, politics and public*. London: Methuen, 1968.

STEINER, George: 'The future of the book: classic culture and past culture'. *Times literary supplement* 2 October, 1970: 1121-3.

STEINER, George: *Language and silence*. Harmondsworth (Middlx): Penguin Books, 1969.

SWEENEY, Francis, *editor: The knowledge explosion*. New York: Farrar, Strans and Giroux, 1966.

UNESCO: *Communications satellites for education, science and culture*. Paris: Unesco, 1967.

UNESCO: *Statistical yearbook*. Paris: Unesco.

UNESCO: *World communications*. Paris: Unesco, 1964.

VOORHEES, R: 'What is television doing to our public libraries' *Library journal* 76: 1951: 567-73.

WARNER, Malcolm: *The data bank society: organizations, computers and social freedom*. London: Allen and Unwin, 1970.

WENNERBURG, U: 'Using the Delphi technique in planning the future of libraries'. *Unesco bulletin for libraries* 26: (5): September-October, 1972: 242: 45.

WESTIN, Alan F: *Information technology in a democracy*. Cambridge (Mass): Harvard University Press, 1971.

WHALE, John: *The half-shut eye: television and politics in Britain*. London: MacMillan, 1967.

WILLIAMS, Francis: *The right to know*. London: Longmans, 1969.

WILSON, Alex: 'Public libraries in the service of leisure' *Journal of librarianship* 4: (4): October, 1972.

WILSON, Charles: *Parliaments peoples and the mass media*. London: Cassell, 1970.

Name and subject index